Lights, Camera, Poetry!

American Movie Poems,

the First Hundred Years

EDITED BY

Jason Shinder

A Harvest Original
Harcourt Brace & Company
San Diego New York London

Requests for permission to make copies of any part of the work
should be mailed to: Permissions Department,
Harcourt Brace & Company, 6277 Sea Harbor Drive,
Orlando, Florida 32887-6777.

Library of Congress Cataloging-in-Publication Data
Lights, camera, poetry: American poets write about the movies/
[edited by] Jason Shinder.—1st ed.
p. cm.
"A Harvest original."
ISBN 0-15-600115-2
1. Motion pictures—Poetry. 2. American poetry—20th century.
I. Shinder, Jason, 1955- .
PS595.M68L54 1996
811'.5080357—dc20   95-45538

Text set in Walbaum
Designed by Kaelin Chappell
Printed in the United States of America
First edition
E D C B A

Permission acknowledgments appear on pages 179–85,
which constitute a continuation of the copyright page.

for Sophie Cabot Black

Contents

Introduction xv

Robert Frost, 1874–1963 Provide, Provide 1

Carl Sandburg, 1878–1967 In a Breath 2

Vachel Lindsay, 1879–1931 Mae Marsh, Motion Picture Actress 3

Archibald MacLeish, 1892–1982 Cinema of a Man 4

e. e. cummings, 1894–1962 death is more than 6

Hart Crane, 1899–1932 Chaplinesque 7

Langston Hughes, 1902–1967 Movies 8

Kenneth Fearing, 1902–1961 Mrs. Fanchier at the Movies 9

Stanley Kunitz, 1905– The Magic Curtain 10

Theodore Roethke, 1908–1963 Double Feature 13

George Oppen, 1908–1984 Travelogue 15

Robert Fitzgerald, 1910–1985 Cinema 16

Ben Belitt, 1911– Soundstage 17

Paul Goodman, 1911–1972 A Documentary Film of Churchill 19

Jean Garrigue, 1912–1972 Movie Actors Scribbling Letters Very Fast in Crucial Scenes 20

Muriel Rukeyser, 1913–1980 Movie 21

Robert Hayden, 1913–1980 Double Feature 22

May Swenson, 1913–1989 The James Bond Movie 23

Karl Shapiro, 1913– Hollywood 24

Delmore Schwartz, 1913–1966 Love and Marilyn Monroe 27

Weldon Kees, 1914–1955 Subtitle 28

John Berryman, 1914–1972 Homage to Film 29

Randall Jarrell, 1914–1965 from "The Lost World" 30

Margaret Walker, 1915– from "On Youth and Age" 31

Robert Lowell, 1917–1977 Harpo Marx 32

William Jay Smith, 1918– Movies for the Troops 33

Robert Duncan, 1919– Ingmar Bergman's *Seventh Seal* 34

Amy Clampitt, 1920–1994 *The Godfather* Returns to Color TV 36

Barbara Guest, 1920– from "Motion Pictures" 37

Richard Wilbur, 1921– *The Prisoner of Zenda* 38

Howard Moss, 1922–   Horror Movie 39
Jack Kerouac, 1922–1969   To Harpo Marx 41
Denise Levertov, 1923–   The Film 42
Louis Simpson, 1923–   "Why don't you get transferred,
Dad?" 43
Alan Dugan, 1923–   Homo Ludens: On an Argument
with an Actor 44
Edward Field, 1924–   Dietrich 45
Jane Cooper, 1924–   Seventeen Questions about
King Kong 46
Stanley Moss, 1925–   Prayer for Zero Mostel
(1915–1977) 48
Frank O'Hara, 1926–1966   Ave Maria 49
Allen Ginsberg, 1926–   The Blue Angel 51
Robert Creeley, 1926–   The Movie Run Backward 53
John Ashbery, 1927–   Farm Film 54
Paul Carroll, 1927–   Ode to Fellini on Interviewing
Actors for a Forthcoming
Film 55
Maya Angelou, 1928–   Miss Scarlett, Mr. Rhett and Other
Latter-Day Saints 56
Irving Feldman, 1928–   Or Perhaps It's Really *Theater* 58
Adrienne Rich, 1929–   Images for Godard 60
John Hollander, 1929–   The Movie 63
Gregory Corso, 1930–   Errol Flynn—On His Death 64
David Ray, 1932–   Movies 65
Amiri Baraka, 1934–   Jim Brown on the Screen 67
John Updike, 1932–   Movie House 69
Linda Pastan, 1932–   Popcorn 70
Michael McClure, 1932–   La Plus Blanche 71
Ted Berrigan, 1934–1983   from "The Sonnets," XXXVIII 72
Grace Schulman, 1935–   The Movie 73
Russell Edson, 1935–   Making a Movie 75
Colleen J. McElroy, 1935–   For the Black Rider of the Black
Hills and Afternoons of Saturday
Matinees at the Antioch
Theatre 76

Richard Brautigan, 1935–1984   The Sidney Greenstreet Blues   78
Lucille Clifton, 1936–   note, passed to superman   79
C. K. Williams, 1936–   Nostalgia   81
Marvin Bell, 1937–   On Location   82
Diane Wakoski, 1937–   Waiting for the New Tom Cruise
    Movie: Summer '88   83
David Meltzer, 1937–   15th Raga / For Bela Lugosi   86
Ishmael Reed, 1938–   Life Is a Screwball Comedy   87
Charles Simic, 1938–   Position without a Magnitude   89
Michael S. Harper, 1938–   Afterword: A Film   90
Al Young, 1939–   W. H. Auden & Mantan
    Moreland   92
Clark Coolidge, 1939–   Three Thousand Hours of Cinema
    by Jean-Luc Godard   93
Stephen Dunn, 1939–   An American Film   95
Robert Pinsky, 1940–   Picture   97
Stephen Dobyns, 1941–   What You Have Come to
    Expect   98
Bob Dylan, 1941–   Brownsville Girl   100
   & Sam Shepard, 1943–
Tom Clark, 1941–   Final Farewell   104
Robert Hass, 1941–   Heroic Simile   105
Sharon Olds, 1942–   The Death of Marilyn Monroe   107
Stan Rice, 1942–   Necking at the Drive-in
    Movie   108
William Matthews, 1942–   Sympathetic   109
Ellen Bryant Voigt, 1943–   At the Movie: Virginia, 1956   110
Laurel Blossom, 1943–   Checkpoint   113
Laurence Goldstein, 1943–   In Person: Bette Davis   114
Terry Stokes, 1943–   Mentioning James Dean   116
Ira Sadoff, 1945–   Take One   118
Carol Muske, 1945–   Last Take   119
Bruce Smith, 1946–   Movies   121
Wanda Coleman, 1946–   Casting Call   123
Ai, 1947—   James Dean   124
Charlie Smith, 1947–   Character Part   127

Albert Goldbarth, 1948–   A Film   129

David Lehman, 1948–   Toward a Definition of Love   130

Ntozake Shange, 1948–   from "mesl (male english as a
second language): in defense of
bilingualism"   133

Steven Bauer, 1948–   The Man Who Knew Too
Much   134

Mark Rudman, 1948–   Cheyenne   135

Bruce Springsteen, 1949–   Be True   137

Denis Johnson, 1949–   Movie within a Movie   138

Mark Doty, 1949–   Adonis Theater   140

Lynn Emanuel, 1949–   Blond Bombshell   143

Marie Howe, 1950–   In the Movies   144

Edward Hirsch, 1950–   The Skokie Theatre   145

Jorie Graham, 1951–   from "Fission"   146

Jim Carroll, 1951–   Living at the Movies   147

Nicholas Christopher, 1951—   Film Noir   149

Jimmy Santiago Baca, 1952–   Main Character   151

David Mura, 1952–   from "Pasolini:" 2 Ninetto at
Evening   152

Ana Castillo, 1953–   Seduced by Natassja Kinski   154

David Trinidad, 1953–   Things to Do in *Valley of the Dolls*
(The Movie)   156

Elaine Equi, 1953–   The Most Beautiful Blonde in the
World   157

Tino Villanueva, 1954–   The 8 O'Clock Movie   158

Louise Erdrich, 1954–   Dear John Wayne   160

Michael Warr, 1954–   Die Again Black Hero:
Version II   162

Thylias Moss, 1954–   Hattie and the Power of
Biscuits   163

Patricia Smith, 1955–   Why I Like Movies   164

Jason Shinder, 1955–   Dark Palace   166

Lucie Brock-Broido, 1956–   So Long, I've Had You Fame   169

Dionisio D. Martinez, 1956–   Reenactments   171

Amy Gerstler, 1956–   Slowly I Open My Eyes   172

ix

Lewis Buzbee, 1957–   Sunday, Tarzan in His
                                      Hammock   173

Diann Blakely Shoaf, 1957–   Reunion Banquet, Class of '79   174
Elise Paschen, 1959–   Red Lanterns   176
Tom Andrews, 1961–   Cinema Vérité: The River of
                                      Barns   177

Permissions   179
Index of Movie Titles and Movie   186
    People
Index of Authors and Poem   188
    Titles

Introduction

I often wonder how I find myself watching another movie.

Indeed, I often find it unexpectedly difficult to remember, in detail, how I started out the day, how I got from my house to work, how I got from work to the movie theater, how I chose this movie over another.

Yet my reaction is always a comfort to me when I finally enter the movie house. The brightly lit candy counter, the popping of the hard corn kernels, the musty aroma of the butter, the thick black liqueur of the Coca-Cola are all so familiar that I feel welcomed, as if coming home. Then I can begin to let go of the day's tiredness, frustrations, and confusions, both real and imagined. I imagine, in fact, that the other people walking into the movie house experience the same sense of comfort, helping deepen, in some mysterious, universal way, our affections for each other.

When I enter the theater, I have a habit of sitting in the aisle seat of the third row, right hand round a large container of popcorn, left hand round a large cup of soda, with a pleased, satisfied expression on my face. Just then, the last waves of the confusion and uneasiness subside, and I can finally rest.

The people behind me begin to talk excitedly about one thing, then another, their voices becoming softer in anticipation, with a faint melody in them, as the houselights go from white to off-white to yellow to black. It is, for a time, very relaxing, and also faintly, mockingly conspiratorial, as if I and everyone else in the theater are partners in league against the difficult, boring, and bright world outside. I am puffed up with a kind of pleasure because we are all seemingly determined to dedicate our energies to becoming part of something livelier, scarier, funnier, if not better, than life.

Do the movie stars realize how hard we are trying to join them, awash in the light of their lives and dramas instead of our own? Their efforts to act on our behalf often make us feel recognized, as if for the first time, as characters full of unspoken passions, talents, and fantasies.

The truth is I'm a movieholic, often seeing three or four movies a week. The films I see are so varied in temperament and ambition, from kung fu action adventures to realistic slices-of-life, that I wonder how they can all be of interest.

It feels as if each movie is a prelude to something better: a more intense life than the one I'm living. It makes no difference whether I see an entire film or just a half hour of it. I seem to be saying: Give me the present. Give me everything happening at once. And give it to me now. Just a few minutes in the dark of a movie theater every other day or so satisfies my addiction.

But sometimes my need for movies is so great it seems it can never be fully satisfied—at least not in the way I imagine satisfying it: sitting across from Marlon Brando, searching his face for just the right inflection and understanding; lying on a lounge chair in sunny Miami beside Jessica Lange; talking from a phone booth to Alfred Hitchcock in the middle of the night; offering up an hysterical line or two to Richard Pryor in the comfort of a stretch limousine.

I did, however, find poems, beautiful poems, in which the movies kept surfacing.

As often happens, I find that through reading poems, with their deep illuminations and rhythms, I begin to better understand and reconcile my own needs and obsessions. The movie poems I discovered helped me to dig deeper for the reasons I first fell in love with the movies, to which I have become utterly attached.

The catalysts for the poems in this collection are numerous and varied. They include the adoration of a movie star, director, or film; the fascination with the internal and external architecture of movie theaters; the simultaneous distance and closeness between actors and moviegoers; Hollywood's treatment of race and gender; the perceived loneliness of an aging movie hero; and, of course, the place of the written word in the age of celluloid.

Many of the poems also represent the influence of cinema on the technique and substance of poetry writing. Beginning with Carl Sandburg's "In a Breath," several of the poems frame observations or descriptions in the same way that movies often show a quick series of scenes, one after another, with little or no transition. Poems such as Clark Coolidge's "Three Thousand Hours of Cinema by Jean-Luc Godard" or Tom Andrews's "Cinema Vérité: The River of Barns" mimic the structure and language of screenplays and moviemaking. In fact, some of the themes addressed in the poems included here would probably never have arisen were it not for the movies.

Interestingly, I discovered that several of the anthologized poets have also been screenwriters, actors, or part of a film's production team. Vachel Lindsay, one of the first American poets to give the cinema serious poetic treatment, wrote the first book of film theory to be published in the English language and wrote several screenplays. Wanda Coleman worked for many years as a casting director. Jim Carroll helped write the screenplay for the feature film based on his coming-of-age memoir, *Basketball Diaries.* Ntozake Shange has written and directed several short films. (Strangely, the poet James Agee, who wrote some of our county's most innovative film reviews and screenplays, including *The African Queen,* wrote no poetry directly about the movies.)

I also found that the lyrics to many songs about the movies contain some of the properties of our liveliest poems. I've included two of these: Bruce Springsteen's "Be True," which uses the movies as a metaphor for describing the differences between a real and imagined relationship, and "Brownsville Girl" by Bob Dylan and Sam Shepard, a large, digressive, intimate musing on the allure of Gregory Peck.

As I reread the anthologized poems, I find they often seem illuminated by something deeper, beyond the poet's fascination for a particular movie or movie star. I understand the source of this illumination to be Hollywood: a central symbol of the uneasy, impossible-to-fulfill longing for everlasting fame, glamour, and love. At the same time, Hollywood figures in the poet's work as a symbol of the difficult, often corrupt compromises one must make to achieve such a high level of notoriety.

By communicating in a language that can speak to people of all ages and backgrounds, movies have become a universal metaphor for how we experience living, especially our need for transformation and transcendence amidst the often difficult conditions of our lives. "The last century discovered electricity," D. W. Griffith explains in a 1920 screenwriting handbook. "In this century movies will discover life."

Indeed. Today, in America, there are movie theaters in every city and in almost every town. Each year millions of Americans wait in line to see the latest action, comedy, drama, or romance on screen. Film studies is one of the fastest growing subjects at college campuses and is now part of the curriculum at a number of high schools. Every major newspaper and magazine features regular film reviews, often by full-time movie critics. "Film has all the fascinating charm of youth" D. W. Griffith declares. "It *is* democracy."

Lights, Cameras, Poetry! is the first book to represent poetry on the movies written exclusively by American poets. As the cinema is just over a hundred years old, this book is also a celebration of a period of poets and poetry associated with the movies.

The poets are arranged chronologically so the reader may trace the development of the movie theme throughout this century. I hope the chronological order will illuminate the subtle and dramatic changes in form and content, as well as the constants of passion and honesty, that distinguish this rich and dynamic period of American poetry.

The poems I have selected represent a small part of a larger and rapidly growing body of work. Because of space constraints, I have limited the collection to shorter movie poems and to sections, where appropriate, of longer poems on the subject. I have also scattered throughout the book a handful of amusing and insightful references to the movies from various writers and works to further illuminate the relationship between writers, poetry, and the movies.

I hope this volume will encourage readers to seek out the entire poems from which sections were taken, other poetry by the anthologized poets, and other books on the subject of movies and writers. Books that have been useful to me in compiling this anthology include *The American Poet at the Movies* by Laurence Goldstein (Ann Arbor: University of Michigan Press, 1994), *The Faber Book of Movie Verse,* edited by Philip French and Ken Wlaschin (London: Faber and Faber, 1993), and *The Movie That Changed My Life,* edited by David Rosenberg (New York: Viking Penguin, 1991).

I am grateful to the many people who provided new insights into the poems I was considering for this collection, and to the many poets, editors, teachers, and friends who brought movie poems to my attention. Special thanks to Laurence Goldstein for his extensive collection of essays on the subject of poets and the movies and for his ongoing support and insights.

Thanks also to Steven Bauer, Sophie Cabot Black, Laurel Blossom, Lucie Brock-Broido, Marie Howe, Lawrence Joseph, Stanley Kunitz, E. Ethelbert Miller, Sheila Murphy, Adrienne Rich, and Alice Quinn. My thanks also to Fred Courtright, permissions editor of this collection, and to Ruth Greenstein, the book's editor at Harcourt Brace, whose invaluable support grows with every anthology we work on together. Thanks, finally, to the poets for their poems and to the people who granted me permission to reprint them.

"In the year 1887, the idea occurred to me that it was possible to devise an instrument which should do for the eye what the phonograph does for the ear, and that by a combination of the two, all motion and sound could be recorded and reproduced simultaneously."

"Inventors must be poets so that they may have imagination."

— THOMAS A. EDISON

ROBERT
FROST

*Provide,
Provide*

The witch that came (the withered hag)
To wash the steps with pail and rag,
Was once the beauty Abishag,

The picture pride of Hollywood.
Too many fall from great and good
For you to doubt the likelihood.

Die early and avoid the fate.
Or if predestined to die late,
Make up your mind to die in state.

Make the whole stock exchange your own!
If need be occupy a throne,
Where nobody can call *you* crone.

Some have relied on what they knew;
Others on being simply true.
What worked for them might work for you.

No memory of having starred
Atones for later disregard,
Or keeps the end from being hard.

Better to go down dignified
With boughten friendship at your side
Than none at all. Provide, provide!

CARL
SANDBURG

In a Breath

High noon. White sun flashes on the Michigan Avenue asphalt. Drum of hoofs and whirr of motors. Women traipesing along in flimsy clothes catching play of sun-fire to their skin and eyes. Inside the playhouse are movies from under the sea. From the heat of pavements and the dust of sidewalks, passers-by go in a breath to be witnesses of huge cool sponges, large cool fishes, large cool valleys and ridges of coral spread silent in the soak of the ocean floor thousands of years.

A naked swimmer dives. A knife in his right hand shoots a streak at the throat of a shark. The tail of the shark lashes. One swing would kill the swimmer.... Soon the knife goes into the soft underneck of the veering fish.... Its mouthful of teeth, each tooth a dagger itself, set row on row, glistens when the shuddering, yawning cadaver is hauled up by the brothers of the swimmer.

Outside in the street is the murmur and singing of life in the sun— horses, motors, women traipesing along in flimsy clothes, play of sun-fire in their blood.

VACHEL
LINDSAY

*Mae Marsh,
Motion Picture
Actress*

(In *Man's Genesis,
The Wild Girl of the Sierras,
The Wharf Rat, A Girl
of the Paris Streets*, etc.)

I

The arts are old, old as the stones
From which man carved the sphinx austere.
Deep are the days the old arts bring:
Ten thousand years of yesteryear.

II

She is madonna in an art
As wild and young as her sweet eyes:
A frail dew flower from this hot lamp
That is today's divine surprise.

Despite raw lights and gloating mobs
She is not seared: a picture still:
Rare silk the fine director's hand
May weave for magic if he will.

When ancient films have crumbled like
Papyrus rolls of Egypt's day,
Let the dust speak: "Her pride was high,
All but the artist hid away:

"Kin to the myriad artist clan
Since time began, whose work is dear."
The deep new ages come with her,
Tomorrow's years of yesteryear.

3

ARCHIBALD
MACLEISH

Cinema of
a Man

The earth is bright through the boughs of the moon like a dead planet
It is silent it has no sound the sun is on it
It shines in the dark like a white stone in a deep meadow
It is round above it is flattened under with shadow

He sits in the rue St. Jacques at the iron table
It is dusk it is growing cold the roof stone glitters on the gable
The taxis turn in the rue du Pot de Fer
The gas jets brighten one by one behind the windows of the stair

This is his face the chin long the eyes looking

Now he sits on the porch of the Villa Serbelloni
He is eating white bread and brown honey
The sun is hot on the lake there are boats rowing
It is spring the rhododendrons are out the wind is blowing

Above Bordeaux by the canal
His shadow passes on the evening wall
His legs are crooked at the knee he has one shoulder
His arms are long he vanishes among the shadows of the alder.

He wakes in the Grand Hotel Vierjahreszeiten
It is dawn the carts go by the curtains whiten
He sees her yellow hair she has neither father nor mother
Her name is Ann she has had him now and before another

This is his face in the light of the full moon
His skin is white and grey like the skin of a quadroon
His head is raised to the sky he stands staring
His mouth is still his face is still his eyes are staring

He walks with Ernest in the streets in Saragossa
They are drunk their mouths are hard they say *qué cosa*
They say the cruel words they hurt each other
Their elbows touch their shoulders touch their feet go on and on
    together

Now he is by the sea at St.-Tropez
The pines roar in the wind it is hot it is noonday
He is naked he swims in the blue under the sea water
His limbs are drowned in the dapple of sun like the limbs of the sea's
    daughter

Now he is in Chicago he is sleeping
The footstep passes on the stone the roofs are dripping
The door is closed the walls are dark the shadows deepen
His head is motionless upon his arm his hand is open

Those are the cranes above the Karun River
They fly across the night their wings go over
They cross Orion and the south star of the Wain
A wave has broken in the sea beyond the coast of Spain

E. E. CUMMINGS

death is

more than

death is more than
certain a hundred these
sounds crowds odours it

is in a hurry
beyond that any this
taxi smile or angle we do

not sell and buy
things so necessary as
is death and unlike shirts
neckties trousers
we cannot wear it out

no sir which is why
granted who discovered
America ether the movies
may claim general importance

to me to you nothing is
what particularly
matters hence in a

little sunlight and less
moonlight ourselves against the worms

hate laugh shimmy

HART
CRANE

Chaplinesque

We make our meek adjustments,
Contented with such random consolations
As the wind deposits
In slithered and too ample pockets.

For we can still love the world, who find
A famished kitten on the step, and know
Recesses for it from the fury of the street,
Or warm torn elbow coverts.

We will sidestep, and to the final smirk
Dally the doom of that inevitable thumb
That slowly chafes its puckered index toward us,
Facing the dull squint with what innocence
And what surprise!

And yet these fine collapses are not lies
More than the pirouettes of any pliant cane;
Our obsequies are, in a way, no enterprise.
We can evade you, and all else but the heart:
What blame to us if the heart live on.

The game enforces smirks; but we have seen
The moon in lonely alleys make
A grail of laughter of an empty ash can,
And through all sound of gaiety and quest
Have heard a kitten in the wilderness.

LANGSTON
HUGHES

Movies

The Roosevelt, Renaissance, Gem, Alhambra:
Harlem laughing in all the wrong places
          at the crocodile tears
          of crocodile art
          that you know
          in your heart
          is crocodile:

          (Hollywood
          laughs at me,
          black—
          so I laugh
          back.)

KENNETH
FEARING

Mrs. Fanchier
at the Movies

If I could reply, but once, to these many new and kindly companions I
    have found
(Now that so many of the old are gone, so far and for so long)
Overhearing them on the radio or the phonograph, or here in the
    motion pictures, as now—

These electrical voices, so sure in the sympathy they extend,
Offering it richly through the long hours of the day and the longer
    hours of the night

(Closer at hand, and although automatic, somehow more
    understanding than a live friend)
Speaking sometimes to each other, but often straight at me—

Wishing I could reply, if only once,
Add somehow to the final burst of triumphant music, or even in tragedy
    mingle with the promise of the fading clouds—

But wondering, too, what it really was I at one time felt so deeply for,
The actual voice, or this muted thunder? These giant shadows, or the
    naked face?
Or something within the voice and behind the face?—

And wondering whether, now, I would have the courage to reply, in
    fact,
Or any longer know the words, or even find the voice.

*The Magic
Curtain*

1

At breakfast Mother sipped her buttermilk,
  her mind already on her shop,
  unrolling gingham by the yard,
stitching her dresses for the Boston trade.
Behind her, Frieda with the yellow hair,
  capricious keeper of the toast,
  buckled her knees, as if she'd lost
balance and platter, then winked at me, blue-eyed.
Frieda, my first love! who sledded me to sleep
  through snows of the Bavarian woods
  into the bell-song of the girls,
with kinds of kisses Mother would not dream;
tales of her wicked stepfather, a dwarf,
  from whom she fled to Bremerhaven
  with scarcely the tatters on her back;
riddles, nonsense, lieder, counting-songs. . . .
  Eins, zwei, drei, vier, fünf, sechs, sieben,
  Wo ist denn mein liebster Herr geblieben?
  Er ist nicht hier, er ist nicht da,
  Er ist fort nach Amerika.
"Be sure," said Mother briskly at the door,
  "that you get Sonny off to school
  on time. And see that he combs his hair."
How could she guess what we two had in mind?

2

Downtown at the Front St. Bi-jo (spelt Bijou)
  we were, as always, the first in line,
  with a hot nickel clutched in hand,
impatient for *The Perils of Pauline,*
my Frieda in her dainty blouse and skirt,
  I in my starched white sailor suit
  and buttoned shoes, prepared to hang

from cliffs, twist on a rack, be tied to rails.
School faded out at every morning reel,
             The Iron Claw held me in thrall,
             Cabiria taught me the Punic Wars,
at bloody Antietam I fought on Griffith's side.
And Keystone Kops came tumbling on the scene
             in outsized uniforms, moustached,
             their thick-browed faces dipped in flour,
to crank tin lizzies that immediately collapsed.
John Bunny held his belly when he laughed,
             ladies politely removed their hats,
             Cyrus of Persia stormed the gates,
upsetting our orgy at Belshazzar's Feast.
Then Charlie shuffled in on bunioned feet.
             We twirled with him an imaginary cane
             and blew our noses for the gallant poor
who bet on a horse, the horse that always loses.
Blanche Sweet, said Frieda, had a pretty name,
             but I came back with Arline Pretty,
             and, even sweeter, Louise Lovely.
Send me your picture, Violet Mersereau!
Lights up! Ushers with atomizers ranged
             the aisles, emitting lilac spray.
             We lunched on peanuts and Hershey bars
and moved to the Majestic for the two o'clock show.

3

Five . . . four . . . three . . . two . . . one . . .
             The frames are whirling backward, see!
             The operator's lost control.
Your story flickers on your bedroom wall.
Deaths, marriages, betrayals, lies,
             close-ups of tears, forbidden games,
             spill in a montage on a screen,
with chases, pratfalls, custard pies, and sores.

You have become your past, which time replays,
        to your surprise, as comedy.
        That coathanger neatly whisked your coat
right off your back. Soon it will want your skin.
        Five . . . four . . . three . . . two . . . one . . .
        Where has my dearest gone?
        She is nowhere to be found,
        She dwells in the underground,
Let the script revel in tricks and transformations.
        When the film is broken, let it be spliced
        where Frieda vanished one summer night
with somebody's husband, daddy to a brood.
And with her vanished, from the bureau drawer,
        the precious rose-enameled box
        that held those chestnut-colored curls
clipped from my sorrowing head when I was four.
After the war an unsigned picture-card
        from Dresden came, with one word: *Liebe.*
        "I'll never forgive her," Mother said,
but as for me, I do and do and do.

T H E O D O R E
R O E T H K E

Double Feature

With Buck still tied to the log, on comes the light.
Lovers disengage, move sheepishly toward the aisle
With mothers, sleep-heavy children, stale perfume, past
    the manager's smile
Out through the velvety chains to the cool air of night.

I dawdle with groups near the rickety pop-corn stand;
Dally at shop windows, still reluctant to go;
I teeter, heels hooked on the curb, scrape a toe;
Or send off a car with vague lifts of a hand.

A wave of Time hangs motionless on this particular shore.
I notice a tree, arsenical grey in the light, or the slow
Wheel of the stars, the Great Bear glittering colder than snow,
And remember there was something else I was hoping for.

"Garbo released from the screen the first intimation of screen beauty. Screen? This was a veil, curiously embroidered, the veil before the temple."

—H. D.

GEORGE
OPPEN

Travelogue

But no screen would show
The light, the volume
Of the moment, or our decisions

In the dugouts, roaring
Downstream with the mud and rainfalls to emergencies
Of village skills and the aboriginal flash

Or handsome paddles among the bright rocks
And channels of the savage country.

ROBERT
FITZGERALD

Cinema

A square of sucking brilliance in the dark.
Over it in the depth and distance a rider
Leaving a comet's furrow of dust. Blink:
Down the gigantic mountain the booted daredevil
Twists the piebald, making play with his bridle:
The savior of the overland stage.
                                        Why, ma'am,
That wasn't no ride at all. Well, Miss Ginger,
Guess I aint ever seen a gal so purty.

Gingham rounded, the breathing bosom shows
Under tight hands. Nearer, the forms distend.
Smooth and vast, her yielding visage slopes
Backward and opens: cheekbones and mouth-molding,
Temples and wide eyes: the beseeching gaze
Casts from eye to eye of the dauntless hero:
Is it love? Oh, is it love, Dusty?
Fuses at last in obliterating clinch.

Matinee: a nickel. The outside, acid air
Alien and cold. Twilight and lights downtown.
Pedestrians huddled in their hurrying strangeness.
Phantasms draining from the ominous world,
Sang froid from the doped urchin. The way home.

BEN
BELITT

Soundstage

*U.S. Signal Corps
Photographic Center: 1945*

1

Catwalk, backdrop, cable, girder, fly—
A schooner capsized:
                    Sea-fans of artifice
Buoyed in the middle currents; gelatin and foil;
Baskets of radiant cordage, geysers of frost,
Miraculous canvas in the glowing levels, glazed,
The backdrops weedy, like oil:
                            The ropes plunge and are lost;
Are parted like hair,
Where, at the summit, among crucibles of light,
Equilibrist Gulliver
Calls to the carpenters in a tightwire vertigo,
At the Archimedean center of deception, unamazed.

And all that is, is film; film is
The serpent in Eden Garden, the cord in the chrysalis,
The bough in the dove's beak trying the deluge,
The thread in the labyrinth
The great wall of China spanning the dynasties
Like a calligraphic symbol; meridians, staves,
Between the upper and nether icecaps; trajectory
Of shell and tracer-bullet, phosphor and satchel-charge;
The looped "I" given to the paper poorly on the burning tripod

And the victory over horror in an image.

2

The boy in the uniform of Oberleutnant, the demoniac flier,
Will not bleed humanly from the papier-mâché doorway.
                                        The door
Will not close truly on the plausible flight,
With leisure for vanity, vacancy, mania, the stunned
  recognition.

17

And mocking the human wish for asylum,
Spray-gun and saw, the jaw of the plier,
Have outpaced fable.

It is divertissement, after all.
What is stilted in canvas, jailed to the plywood wall,
Stabbed to the floor
With wing-screws and metal angles,
Melts into vaudeville in a whirr of velocipedes
And a yelping of trained poodles,
A swindle of spangles.
Only the scaffold gives stress to the weightless interior
On the wrong side of the pattern: the artisan's touch of the
    actual.

3

Yet teased out of thought,
The smiling divination of the Spool
Whirls forever in the large eye of Keats, heavy with film.
For even that Attic shape,
The bride of quietness brought to bed on the urn,
Was not more actual than this.
                              And, in equivocal distance,
Necessitous armies close, image and spectacle wait,
And beat on the canvas door;
The fiction
Calls in the ripening crystal to existence,
Loud as myself—
                in deed, in ghost—
And bleeds in Agamemnon's color,
And is articulate.

PAUL
GOODMAN

A Documentary Film of Churchill

These images are a remarkable
recapitulation, to again
watch the wars and listen to the men
not making sense. Wilson and Churchill
and Roosevelt, resolute and even noble
in their delusions, until on the screen
victory fades into the next war, and vain
policy bursts quietly a bubble.

What is it with this race that does not learn?
I am weary for meaning and they tire
my soul with great deeds. Yet I cannot turn
my eyes from the stupid story in despair:
since I have undertaken to be born,
Adam, Adam is my one desire.

**JEAN
GARRIGUE**

Movie Actors Scribbling Letters Very Fast in Crucial Scenes

The velocity with which they write—
Don't you know it? It's from the heart!
They are acting the whole part out.
Love! has taken them up—
Like writing to god in the night.
Meet me! I'm dying! Come at once!
The crisis is on them, the shock
Drives from the nerve to the pen,
Pours from the blood into ink.

MURIEL
RUKEYSER

Movie

Spotlight her face   her face has no light in it
touch the cheek with light   inform the eyes
press meanings on those lips.

                     See cities from the air,
fix a cloud in the sky, one bird in the bright air,
one perfect mechanical flower in her hair.

Make your young men ride over the mesquite plains;
produce our country on film : here are the flaming shrubs,
the Negroes put up their hands in Hallelujahs,
the young men balance at the penthouse door.

We focus on the screen : look   they tell us
you are a nation of similar whores   remember the Maine
remember you have a democracy of champagne—

And slowly the female face kisses the young man,
over his face the twelve-foot female head
the yard-long mouth enlarges and yawns
                     The End

Here is a city   here the village grows
here are the rich men standing rows on rows,
but the crowd seeps behind the cowboy the lover the king,
past the constructed sets America rises
the bevelled classic doorways   the alleys of trees are witness
America rises in a wave a mass
pushing away the rot.

              The Director cries Cut!
hoarsely CUT   and the people send pistons of force
crashing against the CUT! CUT! of the straw men.

Light is superfluous upon these eyes,
across our minds push new portents of strength
destroying the sets, the flat faces, the mock skies.

ROBERT
HAYDEN

Double Feature

At Dunbar, Castle or Arcade
we rode with the exotic sheik
through deserts of erotic flowers;
held in the siren madonna's arms
were safe from the bill-collector's power.

Forgave the rats and roaches we
could not defeat, beguiled by jazzbo
strutting of a mouse. And when
the Swell Guy, roused to noblest wrath
shot down all those weakéd men,

Oh how we cheered to see the good we were
destroy the bad we'd never be.
What mattered then the false, the true
at Dunbar, Castle or Arcade,
where we were other for an hour or two?

The James Bond Movie

The popcorn is greasy, and I forgot to bring a Kleenex. A pill that's a bomb inside the stomach of a man inside The Embassy blows up. Eructations of flame, luxurious cauliflowers, giganticize into motion. The entire 29-ft. screen is orange, is crackling flesh and brick bursting, blackening, smithereened. I unwrap a Dentyne and, while jouncing my teeth in rubber-tongue-smarting clove, try with the 2-inch-wide paper to blot butter off my fingers. A bubble-bath, room-sized, in which 14 girls, delectable and sexless, are twist-topped Creamy Freezes, (their blond, red, brown, pinkish, lavendar or silver wiglets screwed that high, and varnished) scrub-tickle a lone male, whose chest has just the right amount and distribution of not too curly hair. He's nervously pretending to defend his modesty. His crotch, below the waterline, is also below the frame—but unsubmerged all 28 slick foamy boobs. Their makeup fails to let the girls look naked. Caterpillar lashes, black and thick, lush lips glossed pink like the gum I pop and chew. Contacts on all the eyes that are mostly blue, they're nose-perfect replicas of each other. I've got most of the grease off and on to this little square of paper. I'm folding it now, making creases with my nails.

KARL SHAPIRO

Hollywood

Farthest from any war, unique in time
Like Athens or Baghdad, this city lies
Between dry purple mountains and the sea.
The air is clear and famous, every day
Bright as a postcard, bringing bungalows
    And sights. The broad nights advertise
For love and music and astronomy.

Heart of a continent, the hearts converge
On open boulevards where palms are nursed
With flare-pots like a grove, on villa roads
Where castles cultivated like a style
Breed fabulous metaphors in foreign stone,
    And on enormous movie lots
Where history repeats its vivid blunders.

Alice and Cinderella are most real.
Here may the tourist, quite sincere at last,
Rest from his dream of travels. All is new,
No ruins claim his awe, and permanence,

Despised like customs, fails at every turn.
    Here where the eccentric thrives,
Laughter and love are leading industries.

Luck is another. Here the bodyguard,
The parasite, the scholar are well paid,
The quack erects his alabaster office,
The moron and the genius are enshrined,
And the mystic makes a fortune quietly;
    Here all superlatives come true
And beauty is marketed like a basic food.

O can we understand it? Is it ours,
A crude whim of a beginning people,
A private orgy in a secluded spot?
Or alien like the word *harem*, or true

Like hideous Pittsburgh or depraved Atlanta?
    Is adolescence just as vile
As this its architecture and its talk?

Or are they parvenus, like boys and girls?
Or ours and happy, cleverest of all?
Yes. Yes. Though glamorous to the ignorant
This is the simplest city, a new school.
What is more nearly ours? If soul can mean
    The civilization of the brain,
This is a soul, a possibly proud Florence.

"You have to remember…the film audience is not an audience that is awake, it is an audience that is dreaming."

— GERTRUDE STEIN

"…I have had a chance to face and recognize the full inconsequence of the Pollyanna greasepaint pinkpoodle paradise with its everlasting stereotyped sunlight and its millions of mechanical accessories and sylphlike robots of the age of celluloid."

— HART CRANE

DELMORE
SCHWARTZ

Love and Marilyn Monroe

(after Spillane)

Let us be aware of the true dark gods
Acknowledging the cache of the crotch
The primitive pure and powerful pink and gray
     private sensitivities
Wincing, marvelous in their sweetness, whence rises
     the future.

Therefore let us praise Miss Marilyn Monroe.
She has a noble attitude marked by pride and candor
She takes a noble pride in the female nature and torso
She articulates her pride with directness and exuberance
She is honest in her delight in womanhood and manhood.
She is not only a great lady, she is more than a lady,
She continues the tradition of Dolly Madison and Clara Bow
When she says, "Any woman who claims she does not like
     to be grabbed is a liar!"
Whether true or false, this colossal remark
     states a dazzling intention . . .

    It might be the birth of a new Venus among us
    It atones at the very least for such as Carrie Nation
    For Miss Monroe will never be a blue nose,
       and perhaps we may hope
    That there will be fewer blue noses because
       she has flourished—
    Long may she flourish in self-delight and the joy
       of womanhood.
    A nation haunted by Puritanism owes her homage and
       gratitude.

Subtitle

We present for you this evening
A movie of death: observe
These scenes chipped celluloid
Reveals unsponsored and tax-free.

We request these things only:
All gum must be placed beneath the seats
Or swallowed quickly, all popcorn sacks
Must be left in the foyer. The doors
Will remain closed throughout
The performance. Kindly consult
Your programs: observe that
There are no exits. This is
A necessary precaution.

Look for no dialogue, or for the
Sound of any human voice: we have seen fit
To synchronize this play with
Squealings of pigs, slow sound of guns,
The sharp dead click
Of empty chocolatebar machines.
We say again: there are
No exits here, no guards to bribe,
No washroom windows.

No finis to the film unless
The ending is your own.
Turn off the lights, remind
The operator of his union card:
Sit forward, let the screen reveal
Your heritage, the logic of your destiny.

J O H N
B E R R Y M A N

Homage
to Film

This night I have seen a film
That might have startled Henry James
From his massive calm
Of discipline, or sent Donne
Into passion, perhaps all names
Of crafty men delighted as the sun.

The sun of another medium
Comes up the East, mechanical
As any art, slow, but it will come
Faster and at last find
Its noon an Argus brain that shall
Center all complexities in mind.

Idiom and reference are but
Statistics of catastrophe,
Intensity is the lever that
Releases ecstasy in the bone
Of all men always, in city,
Hills or in a wilderness of stone.

RANDALL
JARRELL

*from "The
Lost World"*

II. A NIGHT WITH LIONS

When I was twelve we'd visit my aunt's friend
Who owned a lion, the Metro-Goldwyn-Mayer
Lion. I'd play with him, and he'd pretend
To play with me. I was the real player
But he'd trot back and forth inside his cage
Till he got bored. I put Tawny in the prayer
I didn't believe in, not at my age,
But said still; just as I did everything in fours
And gave to Something, on the average,
One cookie out of three. And by my quartz, my ores,
My wood with the bark on it, from the Petrified
Forest, I put his dewclaw . . .
                              Now the lion roars
His slow comfortable roars; I lie beside
My young, tall, brown aunt, out there in the past
Or future, and I sleepily confide
My dream-discovery: my breath comes fast
Whenever I see someone with your skin,
Hear someone with your voice. The lion's steadfast
Roar goes on in the darkness. I have been
Asleep awhile when I remember: you
Are—you, and Tawny was the lion in—
In *Tarzan.* In *Tarzan!* Just as we used to,
I talk to you, you talk to me or pretend
To talk to me as grown-up people do,
Of *Jurgen* and Rupert Hughes, till in the end
I think as a child thinks: "You're my real friend."

from
"On Youth
and Age"

II

This is my century:
Radio and picture-show;
Hot-rod, computer, video;
Ancient, rusty, slow auto:

Ah-ooga, ooga, ooga

Rumble seat and canvas coat.
"All you gals who smoke cigarettes
throw your butts in here."

Ante up the money.
Roll up the screens.
Clones and clowns and robots
Hear the lasers scream.

Soon there won't be any more.
We can't play Popeye and Olive Oyl forever.
Our century is about to expire.

Call the doctor; call the ambulance.
Get the fire department.
Put our feeble century in intensive care.
See if the old man can't last till tomorrow.
Everybody's getting burned up in this fire.

ROBERT
LOWELL

Harpo Marx

Harpo Marx, your hands white-feathered the harp—
the only words you ever spoke were sound.
The movie's not always the sick man of the arts,
yours touched the stars; Harpo, your motion picture
is still life unchanging, not nature dead.
You dumbly memorized an unwritten script . . .
I saw you first two years before you died,
a black-and-white fall, near Fifth in Central Park:
old blond hair too blonder, old eyes too young.
Movie trucks and five police trucks wheel to wheel
like covered wagons. The crowd as much or little.
I wish I had knelt . . . I age to your wincing smile,
like Dante's movie, the great glistening wheel of life—
the genius *happy* . . . a generic actor.

WILLIAM JAY
SMITH

Movies for the Troops

I

In Hollywood the pale white stars
Slump (drunk and jeweled) in Milk Bars,
Or tour the palm-lined avenues
In gently rocking open cars.

II

The burly boys off to the wars
To die (with mention in the news)
Accept these images that fuse,
And clap their hands, and thank their stars.

ROBERT
DUNCAN

*Ingmar
Bergman's
Seventh Seal*

This is the way it is. We see
three ages in one: the child Jesus
innocent of Jerusalem and Rome
—magically at home in joy—
that's the year from which
our inner persistence has its force.

The second, Bergman shows us,
carries forward image after image
of anguish, of the Christ crossd
and sends up from open sores of the plague
(shown as wounds upon His corpse)
from lacerations in the course of love
(the crown of whose kingdom tears the flesh)

. . . There is so much suffering!
What possibly protects us
from the emptiness, the forsaken cry,
the utter dependence, the vertigo?
Why do so many come to love's edge
only to be stranded there?

The second face of Christ, his
evil, his Other, emaciated, pain and sin.
Christ, what a contagion!
What a stink it spreads round

our age! It's our age!
and the rage of the storm is abroad.
The malignant stupidity of statesmen rules.
The old riders thru the forest race
    shouting: the wind! the wind!
Now the black horror cometh again.

And I'll throw myself down
as the clown does in Bergman's *Seventh Seal*
to cower as if asleep with his wife and child,
hid in the caravan under the storm.

Let the Angel of Wrath pass over.
Let the end come.
War, stupidity and fear are powerful.
We are only children. To bed! to bed!
    To play safe!

To throw ourselves down
helplessly, into happiness,
    into an age of our own, into
    our own days.
There where the Pestilence roars,
where the empty riders of the horror go.

AMY
CLAMPITT

The Godfather Returns to Color TV

The lit night glares like a day-glo strawberry,
the stakeout car beside the hydrant is full of feds,
and the ikon of our secret hero(ine?), atop the
feckless funnypaper mesa we try to live in, is that
poor dumb indestructible super-loser Krazy Kat.

O Innocence, spoiled Guinea Brat!—after whose
fits of smashing and screaming, O Holy Mother,
All-American Girl, I need you, I want
to protect you: after that one sunstruck
glimpse, on a Sicilian mountainside,

of virgin stupidity, its sensual lockbox
so charged with possibilities of being
that we too tremble at the thought of nakedness,
of marriage, we too burn to build a shrine for,
raise armies to protect a property that history

godfathered dumb. I told you: DON'T ASK
QUESTIONS ABOUT MY BUSINESS! While the old
bull in a new world, who's lost respect,
too-big pants bunched underneath the belly, stumbles
expiring past the staked tomato vines,

and the grandchild thinks for a minute he's
only playing, we *know* he is, admiring
Marlon Brando in a show of weakness. But the blood
isn't all ketchup, or the weekend all football, nor
do all commodities survive in lighted shrines.

BARBARA
GUEST

*from "Motion
Pictures"*

MOTION PICTURES: 5

It was the scene where the toothy actress takes a glass of water and places it on a table next to a bouquet of flowers; the glass of water was merely a prop intended to remove the camera from her ambitious arrangement of flowers; the camera following the rhythm of the water picked up the shine of her molars as she brought the water to her face disrupting the planned lighting of a fade-out to a mansion where the star of the picture under a canopy of ice green purple red lay chained to an enormous burlap bag with "TROUSERS FOR EXTRAS" written on it; and there were many many people in the chamber all dressed in trousers with "grips" handling extra lights and extra food and extra "quiet" cards for the extra stages in what was to be one of the most gigantic productions of the studio.

RICHARD
WILBUR

The Prisoner
of Zenda

At the end a
The Prisoner of Zenda,
The King being out of danger,
Stewart Granger
(As Rudolph Rassendyll)
Must swallow a bitter pill
By renouncing his co-star,
Deborah Kerr.

It would be poor behavia
In him and in Princess Flavia
Were they to put their own
Concerns before those of the Throne.
Deborah Kerr must wed
The King instead.

Rassendyll turns to go.
Must it be so?
Why can't they have their cake
And eat it, for heaven's sake?

Please let them have it both ways,
The audience prays.
And yet it is hard to quarrel
With a plot so moral.

One redeeming factor,
However, is that the actor
Who plays the once-dissolute King
(Who has learned through suffering
Not to drink or be mean
To his future Queen),
Far from being a stranger,
Is *also* Stewart Granger.

HOWARD
MOSS

Horror Movie

Dr. Unlikely, we love you so,
You who made the double-headed rabbits grow
From a single hare. Mutation's friend,
Who could have prophesied the end
When the Spider Woman deftly snared the fly
And the monsters strangled in a monstrous kiss
And somebody hissed, "You'll hang for this!"?

Dear Dracula, sleeping on your native soil,
(Any other kind makes him spoil),
How we clapped when you broke the French door down
And surprised the bride in the overwrought bed.
Perfectly dressed for lunar research,
Your evening cape added much,
Though the bride, inexplicably dressed in furs,
Was a study in jaded jugulars.

Poor, tortured Leopard Man, you changed your spots
In the debauched village of the Pin-Head Tots;
How we wrung our hands, how we wept
When the eighteenth murder proved inept,
And, caught in the Phosphorous Cave of Sea,
Dangling the last of synthetic flesh,
You said, "There's something wrong with me."

The Wolf Man knew when he prowled at dawn
Beginnings spin a web where endings spawn.
The bat who lived on shaving cream,
A household pet of Dr. Dream,
Unfortunately, maddened by the bedlam,
Turned on the Doc, bit the hand that fed him.

And you, Dr. X, who killed by moonlight,
We loved your scream in the laboratory
When the panel slid and the night was starry

And you threw the inventor in the crocodile pit
(An obscure point: Did he deserve it?)
And you took the gold to Transylvania
Where no one guessed how insane you were.

We thank you for the moral and the mood,
Dear Dr. Cliché, Nurse Platitude.
When we meet again by the Overturned Grave,
Near the Sunken City of the Twisted Mind,
(In *The Son of the Son of Frankenstein*),
Make the blood flow, make the motive muddy:
There's a little death in every body.

JACK
KEROUAC

To Harpo Marx

O Harpo! When did you seem like an angel
    the last time?
    and played the gray harp of gold?

When did you steal the silverware
    and bug-spray the guests?

When did your brother find rain
    in your sunny courtyard?

When did you chase your last blonde
    across the Millionairesses' lawn
    with a bait hook on a line
    protruding from your bicycle?

Or when last you powderpuffed
    your white flour face
    with fishbarrel cover?

Harpo! Who was that Lion
    I saw you with?

How did you treat the midget
    and Konk the Giant?

Harpo, in your recent nightclub appearance
    in New Orleans were you old?
    Were you still chiding with your horn
    in the cane at your golden belt?

Did you still emerge from your pockets
    another Harpo, or screw on
    new wrists?

Was your vow of silence an Indian Harp?

**DENISE
LEVERTOV**

The Film

Turtle Goddess
she of the hard shell
soft underneath
awaits enormously
in a dark grotto
the young Heroes—

Then the corridor
of booths—in each
Life enshrined in
veils of light, scenes
of bliss or
dark action.
Honey and fog, the nose
confused.

And at the corridor's end
two steps
down into Nothing—

The film is over
we're out in the street—

The film-maker's wife grieves and tells him
good-by for ever, you were wrong,
wrong to have shown the Turtle Mother.
The darkness
should not be revealed.
Farewell.

Maker of visions
he walks with me
to the gate of Home and leaves me.
I enter.

Mother is gone,
only Things remain.

So be it.

LOUIS
SIMPSON

"Why don't you get transferred, Dad?"

One of Jimmy's friends comes by in his car,
and Jimmy goes out. "Be careful,"
Mom says. He has to learn to drive,
but it makes her nervous thinking about it.

Darlene goes over to see Marion
whose father is being transferred
to a new branch of the company
in Houston. "Why don't you get transferred, Dad?"

"I'd like to," he replies.
"I'd also like a million dollars."

This is a constant topic in the family:
where else you would like to live.
Darlene likes California—
"It has beautiful scenery
and you get to meet all the stars."
Mom prefers Arizona, because of a picture
she saw once, in *Good Housekeeping.*
Jimmy doesn't care,
and Dad likes it here. "You can find anything
you want right where you are."
He reminds them of *The Wizard of Oz,*
about happiness, how it is found
right in your own backyard.

Dad's right, Mom always says.
The Wizard of Oz is a tradition
in the family. They see it every year.

43

ALAN
DUGAN

Homo Ludens: On an Argument with an Actor

There is a difference between acting and action.
After a bad take the killer and the killed
get up and go back to their chalk marks
and do it over again until the director is satisfied.
Some of us actors claim that action is acting.
This is too simplistic a claim, though true
in a way: we have to pretend to survive,
and stunt men sometimes get maimed or die,
like gladiators in the Roman Games,
but if I shoot you or you shoot me, one
of us winds up in the hospital or morgue
and the other winds up in jail or escapes.
This is the difference between acting and action,
although the deaths of gladiators and stunt men
make a clear definition of the differences difficult.

EDWARD
FIELD

Dietrich

She never had to make up
for not being popular at school—
she started out well beyond all that.

She was never a bobbysoxer, for example,
nor one of those girls fighting
against going all the way—
you don't go from that to where she is.

When she sings *"My ideal is a big blond man"*
or *"Every night another bliss"*
you know just what she means by this.

Ancient in Paris,
perfect setting for monuments
where the boulevards culminate
in a granite bust,

where the populace adores
the will that invents
an inviolable mask—
still she writes "This rotten world,"

as if tied to a mast and forced
to witness, as she always has—
her eyes windows
with the shades permanently up.

JANE
COOPER

Seventeen Questions about King Kong

*The most amazing thing
I know about Jane Cooper
is that she's the niece
of King Kong*

—JAMES WRIGHT

Is it a myth? And if so, what does it tell us about ourselves?

Is Kong a giant ape, or is he an African, beating his chest like a responsive gong?

Fay Wray lies in the hand of Kong as in the hand of God the Destroyer. She gives the famous scream. Is the final conflict (as Merian C. Cooper maintained) really between man and the forces of nature, or is it a struggle for the soul and body of the white woman?

Who was more afraid of the dark, Uncle Merian or his older sister? She was always ready to venture downstairs whenever he heard a burglar.

When he was six his Confederate uncle gave him EXPLORATIONS AND ADVENTURES IN EQUATORIAL AFRICA by Paul du Chaillu, 1861. Does that island of prehistoric life forms still rise somewhere off the coast of the Dark Continent, or is it lost in preconscious memory?

Is fear of the dark the same as fear of sexuality? Mary Coldwell his mother would have destroyed herself had she not been bound by a thread to the wrist of her wakeful nurse. What nights theirs must have been!

Why was I too first called after Mary (or Merian) Coldwell, till my mother, on the morning of the christening, decided it was a hard-luck name?

How does our rising terror at so much violence, as Kong drops the sailors one by one into the void or rips them with his fangs, resolve itself into shame at Kong's betrayal?

Is Kong's violence finally justified, because he was in chains?

Is King Kong our Christ?

Watch him overturn the el-train, rampage through the streets! But why is New York, the technological marvel, so distrusted, when technologically the film was unsurpassed for its time?

Must the anthropologist always dream animal dreams? Must we?

Kong clings to the thread of the Empire State Building. He wavers. Why did Uncle Merian and his partner Schoedsack choose to play the airmen who over and over exult to shoot Kong down?

He said: *Why did I ever leave Africa?*—and then as if someone had just passed a washcloth over his face: *But I've had a very good marriage.*

STANLEY
MOSS

Prayer for
Zero Mostel
(1915–1977)

Señor, already someone else,
O my clown,
the man in your image
was a bestiary,
sweet as sugar,
beautiful as the world,
lizard sitting on a trellis
follows blonde into john,
now a butterfly on the edge
of a black-eyed susan,
rhinoceros
filing down his own horn
for aphrodisiac.
Señor, already someone else,
a band of actors under bombardment
played Shakespeare,
the last few days
of the Warsaw ghetto,
a few of the survivors
who crawled through the sewers
heard the SS was giving out visas
for America
at a certain hotel,
went to apply.

Ave Maria

Mothers of America
                        let your kids go to the movies!
get them out of the house so they won't know what you're up to
it's true that fresh air is good for the body
                                    but what about the soul
that grows in darkness, embossed by silvery images
and when you grow old as grow old you must
                                        they won't hate you
they won't criticize you they won't know
                            they'll be in some glamorous country
they first saw on a Saturday afternoon or playing hookey

they may even be grateful to you
                            for their first sexual experience
which only cost you a quarter
                                and didn't upset the peaceful home
they will know where candy bars come from
                                and gratuitous bags of popcorn
as gratuitous as leaving the movie before it's over
with a pleasant stranger whose apartment is in the
                                    Heaven on Earth Bldg
near the Williamsburg Bridge
                        oh mothers you will have made the little tykes
so happy because if nobody does pick them up in the movies
they won't know the difference
                            and if somebody does it'll be sheer gravy
and they'll have been truly entertained either way
instead of hanging around the yard
                                or up in their room
                                    hating you

prematurely since you won't have done anything horribly
                                    mean yet
except keeping them from the darker joys
                            it's unforgivable the latter

so don't blame me if you won't take this advice

                                        and the family breaks up

and your children grow old and blind in front of a TV set

                                                        seeing

movies you wouldn't let them see when they were young

ALLEN
GINSBERG

The Blue Angel

Marlene Dietrich is singing a lament
for mechanical love.
She leans against a mortarboard tree
on a plateau by the seashore.

She's a life-sized toy,
the doll of eternity;
her hair is shaped like an abstract hat
made out of white steel.

Her face is powdered, whitewashed and
immobile like a robot.
Jutting out of her temple, by an eye,
is a little white key.

She gazes through dull blue pupils
set in the whites of her eyes.
She closes them, and the key
turns by itself.

She opens her eyes, and they're blank
like a statue's in a museum.
Her machine begins to move, the key turns
again, her eyes change, she sings

—you'd think I would have thought a plan
to end the inner grind,
but not till I have found a man
to occupy my mind.

*"What the black actor has managed to give
are moments—indelible moments, created,
miraculously, beyond the confines of the script:
hints of reality, smuggled like contraband into
a maudlin tale, and with enough force, if
unleashed, to shatter the tale to fragments."*

— JAMES BALDWIN

ROBERT
CREELEY

The Movie Run Backward

The words will one day come
back to you, birds returning,
the movie run backward.

Nothing so strange in its talk,
just words. The people
who wrote them are the dead ones.

This here paper talks like anything
but is only one thing,
"birds returning."

You can "run the movie
backward" but "the movie run
backward." The movie run backward.

J O H N
A S H B E R Y

Farm Film

Takeitapart, no one understands how you can just do
This to yourself. Balancing a long pole on your chin
And seeing only the ooze of foliage and blue sunlight
Above. At the same time you have not forgotten

The attendant itch, but, being occupied solely with making
Ends meet, or the end, believe that it will live, raised
In secrecy, into an important yet invisible destiny, unfulfilled.
If the dappled cows and noon plums ever thought of

Answering you, your answer would be like the sun, convinced
It knows best, maybe having forgotten someday. But for this
She looked long for one clothespin in the grass, the rime
And fire of midnight etched each other out, into importance

That is like a screen sometimes. So many
Patterns to choose from, they the colliding of all dispirited
Illustration on our lives, that will rise in its time like
Temperature, and mean us, and then faint away.

Ode to Fellini on Interviewing Actors for a Forthcoming Film

Wasps and flowers fill the 1910 confession box.
    Hot. Hot. But the lovely Witch of the North, wearing
        a Puritan black velvet hat
           and backless black bikini,
peddles slowly on her bicycle about the beach
    at St.-Tropez. Two Mercy nuns, whose fingers stink
        like stale blue milk or Labrador,
           herd us across the schoolyard
protected by the Swiss Guards of the snow;
        we kneel, itching

inside snowsuits, wet, around the marble altar rail.
    Monsignor floats in from the sacristy,
        pressing a glass relic box against
           his belly; we cry and kiss
the hairy knuckle of the virgin martyr. The hands
    of Christ are the muscles of the sun:
        they make flesh and bone from bread
           and blood from ordinary

table wine. There is another moon,
        its slow tides

the menstrual flow of the nuns. Around your office table
    crowd an old alcoholic circus clown,
        a Christmas doll and three umbrellas
           and Anita Ekberg's mother
in a photo. Rain falls on artificial flowers. What
    if everything comes from the sea? The angels
        are ecstatic fish. Or helicopters.
           And you, Fellini, are
a deep-sea diver, searching for the sex
        of God. Good luck.

MAYA
ANGELOU

Miss Scarlett, Mr. Rhett and Other Latter-Day Saints

Novitiates sing Ave
Before the whipping posts,
Criss-crossing their breasts and
tear-stained robes
in the yielding dark.

Animated by the human sacrifice
(Golgotha in black-face)
Priests glow purely white on the
bas-relief of a plantation shrine.

(O Sing)
You are gone but not forgotten
Hail, Scarlett. *Requiescat in pace.*

God-Makers smear brushes in
blood/gall
to etch frescoes on your
ceilinged tomb.

(O Sing)
Hosanna, King Kotton.

Shadowed couplings of infidels
tempt stigmata from the nipples
of your true-believers.

(Chant Maternoster)
Hallowed Little Eva.

Ministers make novena with the
charred bones of four
very small
very black
very young children

(Intone DIXIE)

And guard the relics
of your intact hymen
daily putting to death,
into eternity,
The stud, his seed,
His seed
His seed.

(O Sing)
Hallelujah, pure Scarlett
Blessed Rhett, the Martyr.

IRVING
FELDMAN

Or Perhaps It's Really Theater

Or perhaps it's really *theater* of deprivation,
and here we've wandered onto a movie set
mocked up from famous stills of fifty years ago,
and we're free to walk around and rub elbows with
these lucky white stand-ins* for the tardy stars.
Why, of course, we could be extras here ourselves!
And look, there's the strange moment before the MIRROR,
the gruesome all-nighter around the KITCHEN TABLE,
the DOORWAY where she threw him that funny look
that stayed with him his first weeks off in the army.
At last we'll get to see the backsides of everything,
and find out maybe what really was going on
—no poverty so poor it has no secrets!
And so, having these scenes for our inspection, at
our disposition, is sexy, exciting,
here's fame and nostalgia and something else precious:
seeing the machinery and yet not losing
the illusion . . .

But haven't we seen this flick before?
You know, the one where . . . right out of the 'thirties
. . . the bodies sagging among CHAIRS and WASHSTANDS
or plodding by COFFEE URNS and BUTCHER BLOCKS
through the grainy atmosphere, and gloom that suggests
perpetual confinement to amateurishness
. . . these coercive images of life after hope
. . . a century's terror by sentimentalism
freights the scene with yet blacker glooms of bad faith
—since candor alone is lighthearted—
somewhere a butcher's blunt finger is rending hearts,
while, faint, sweet, *crescendo* from the phantom soundtrack,
the still, sad music of humanism—so-called—
is symphonizing on the dark Stalinist fiddles . . .

*The white stand-ins and the scenes in which they are grouped have been suggested
by the plaster sculptures of George Segal. The "we" are gallery-goers at a show of such
works.

58

Yes, the little people are appealing to *us*
to lead them into history . . . are dying to enlist
in the great cause of our generosity,
and, cap in hand, they come to us and say
with a shy dignity we simply can't resist,
"Here, good sirs, is all of our misery
—do with it, please, as you see fit."
. . . Careers open to idealism!

It all comes back, however faint, that redolence
of another era, but with the smugness cuddly,
the deception almost affectionate, affordable,
almost a joke—somber and improbable camp
that feels right at home in our living room.

Whatever can we be so famished for?

ADRIENNE
RICH

*Images for
Godard*

1. Language as city:: Wittgenstein:
   Driving to the limits
   of the city of words

   the superhighway streams
   like a comic strip

   to newer suburbs
   casements of shockproof glass

   where no one yet looks out
   or toward the coast where even now

   the squatters in their shacks
   await eviction

   When all conversation
   becomes an interview
   under duress

   when we come to the limits
   of the city

   my face must have a meaning

2. To know the extremes of light
   I sit in this darkness

   To see the present flashing
   in a rearview mirror

   blued in a plateglass pane
   reddened in the reflection

   of the red Triomphe
   parked at the edge of the sea

   the sea glittering in the sun
   the swirls of nebula

in the espresso cup
raindrops, neon spectra

on a vinyl raincoat

3. To love, to move perpetually
    as the body changes

    a dozen times a day
    the temperature of the skin

    the feeling of rise & fall
    deadweight & buoyancy

    the eye sunk inward
    the eye bleeding with speech

    for that moment at least
    I was you—

    To be stopped, to shoot the same scene
    over & over

4. At the end of *Alphaville*
    she says *I love you*

    and the film begins
    that you've said you'd never make

    because it's impossible:
    things as difficult to show
    as horror & war & sickness are

    meaning: *love,*
    to speak in the mouth

    to touch the breast
    for a woman

to know the sex of a man
That film begins here

yet you don't show it
we leave the theatre

suffering from that

5. Interior monologue of the poet:
   the notes for the poem are the only poem

   the mind collecting, devouring
   all these destructibles

   the unmade studio couch the air
   shifting the abalone shells

   the mind of the poet is the only poem
   the poet is at the movies

   dreaming the film-maker's dream but differently
   free in the dark as if asleep

   free in the dusty beam of the projector
   the mind of the poet is changing

   the moment of change is the only poem

JOHN
HOLLANDER

The Movie

The old picture plays
Lights across the screen.
Overhead, the beam
From the thoughtful booth
Flickers in a kind
Of code that only
The screen can read out.

Lights like memories
Flicker on the screen
Of your deep gazing.
My eyes and my hand
Are like some part of
The surrounding dark.

Errol Flynn —
On His Death

Good Sea Hawk
you knew the violence & tenderness of this sea
same sea to which the dry huntsman did come
and gather thee

Soft-voiced Velveteer! with buttons snow pronounc'd—
When your wings closed
the winds knocked at another world
Your duelling shadow no longer ballets on the wall
Golden beau of Elizabeth
do you sit among white lions
enamoured by Miss Death
Do you interpret her grapes
Can you care
Can you care if the Spanish Armada recovers

Now your dream companion Alan Hale
comes trudging down the vale
He's weighed with new adventure
and an endless supply of ale
Join him! Together free
the galley slaves of heaven
Lucifer now has need of thee

DAVID
RAY

Movies

for Jane Goodall

We watch *Gorillas in the Mist.*
Evidently it is nicer
to be gorillas
than to be people like us.
The lady was at war with the bad people.
She loved the good gorillas
who beat their chests,
fought for their children,
died trying—but she was no match
of course for the bad people,
which seems to be the case in all
the bad places
that were once paradise. One sees
how hard it is to save anything—
a tree, a tusk, an infant gorilla.
I'm surprised if I can save
from the fire of time one poem,
one shard of the jug we drank from.
The lady flies into a rage—
for they've attacked again,
those with the law on their side.
The grieving babe is carried off
in a crate, another theft
off her sacred mountain.
The bad men want heads for trophies,
babies for zoos, hands for ashtrays—
the hand she held, feeling that touch,
that flow of one being into another
what Michelangelo painted on the ceiling,
scene we must still look up to, something
of the divine. She found it
there in the jungle,
but then the movie is over
and a wise one among us tells us
the lady was not such a nice person.
The lover in the movie was not

her lover. The man that part
was based on said he didn't
even like her and her hair
was always unkempt. She was irrational,
you might say, warring with the locals,
who had to make a living off gorillas.
She had smoked herself so close
to death that her murder was merciful,
a blessing, and so on. It seems
that only in movies heroes
and heroines are perfect. Swift
loved the horses and she
the gorillas we say, and leave it at that.

Jim Brown
on the Screen

is the past in a new package, in daylight sunlight
with the white woman of his savagery done up in brown
for advertising newness in the deadness and liveness
in the oldness, of punctured, rotting, maggot loving A
merica America America, my cunt
tree
what an odd arrangement

of nature, a
cunt
tree
where the "one eyed bird" rules inside the heads of drylipped
slobberers
worshipping the blackwhiteness
of died Ann
Dyed Ann
who they killed anyway and shotup with their bulletejaculation
Dyed Annnnnnnnn who-muh they chang-ed into "dem"
tho she has a sheen of black beneath and makes her anyway more
than they could ever hope to imagine even on the silver screek.
Jim Brown socked them. Socittoembabeeee
He knocked them down. Yea. Bad dude bad dude you dig him crack
that faggot in the mouth . . . yeh (hand slap) 'sa bad motofreaky
Jim Brown put his hand on a white woman . . . youmember he put his
hand on that gray bitch . . . the one with . . . yeh hell yeh, too much
oh man they doin that all overnow . . . Poitier kissed one in the
mirror . . . wat about that time Jimmy Brown kicked that sucker in
the nuts . . . (hand slap) yeh . . . yeh, knocked that motherfucker out

. . . in the space freakout station of our slavery
          mourn for us soldout and chained to devilpictures
          in this cold ass land of ruling doodoo birds and hairy ladies

I mean we walk in whiteness like the rest life sucked out on a
humble death eminent planned by whiteness to the white resolution
of all things. Jim Brown. Our man in space correcting the image
for now, with the old chain of whiteness forever, whiteness, for

ever, if he could escape, if he, could kill them all Jim, killem
Jim if he could, if he could race past any of them, again, like
he used to, in the real world, that image for us to build, among
the easy slickness of imitation, and accommodation. We know you livin
good Jim, we know you walk in stores and buy shit, (hand
slap, stomp, wheel) Yeh, we know you know all kinda hip folks
and talk easy in leather bars, and sashay through parties with
the eyes of our women and beastwomen glued to yo thang, Jim
you can be more than that anyway, more than a new amos in space
more than uncle thomas from inner plantation psychotic
cotton salvation you could be a man, Jim, our man on the land
our new creator and leader, if you would just do it and be it
in the real world
in the new world of yo own black people
I hope you do
it, Jim
I hope you unmaniquin yo
self, you can
do it, if you
want it, you can

you
sho
can, jim

JOHN
UPDIKE

Movie House

View it, by day, from the back,
from the parking lot in the rear,
for from this angle only
the beautiful brick blankness can be grasped.
Monumentality
wears one face in all ages.

No windows intrude real light
into this temple of shades,
and the size of it,
the size of the great rear wall measures
the breadth of the dreams we have had here.

It dwarfs the village bank,
outlooms the town hall,
and even in its decline
makes the bright-ceilinged supermarket seem mean.

Stark closet of stealthy rapture,
vast introspective camera
wherein our most daring self-projections
were given familiar names:
stand, stand by your macadam lake
and tell the aeons of our extinction
that we too could house our gods,
could secrete a pyramid
to sight the stars by.

LINDA
PASTAN

Popcorn

When Plato said
that what we see are shadows
flickering on a cave wall,
he must have meant
the movies.
You let a cigarette lean
from your mouth precisely
as Bogart did.
Because of this, reels later,
we say of our life
that it is B-grade;
that it opened and will close
in a dusty place where
things move always
in slow motion;
that what is real
is the popcorn
jammed between our teeth.

MICHAEL
MCCLURE

La Plus

Blanche

JEAN HARLOW, YOU ARE IN BEAUTY ON DARK
[EARTH WITH WHITE FEET! MICHAEL
slaying the dragon is not more wonderful than you. To air
you give magical sleekness. We shall carry you into Space
on our shoulders. You triumph over all with warm legs and a
smile of wistful anxiety that's cover for the honesty
spoken by your grace! Inner energy presses out to you in
[warmness—

you return love. Love returned for admiration! Strangeness
is returned by you for desire. How. Where
but in the depth of Jean Harlow is such strangeness
made into grace? How many women are more beautiful
in shape and apparition! How few can /have/

draw such love to them? For you are the whole creature of love!

Your muscles are love muscles!

Your nerves—Love nerves!

And your upturned
comic eyes!
Sleep dreams of you.

TED
BERRIGAN

from
"The Sonnets"

XXXVIII

Sleep half sleep half silence and with reasons
For you I starred in the movie
Made on the site
Of Benedict Arnold's triumph, Ticonderoga, and
I shall increase from this
As I am a cowboy and you imaginary
Ripeness begins corrupting every tree
Each strong morning   A man signs a shovel
And so he digs   It hurts   and so
We get our feet wet in air   we love our lineage
Ourselves   Music, salve, pills, kleenex, lunch
And the promise never to truckle   A man
Breaks his arm and so he sleeps   he digs
In sleep half silence and with reason

G R A C E
S C H U L M A N

The Movie

One day I stumbled on a movie set
Of University Place: a surreal park,
A pointillist mews with gleaming iron gates,
Shuttered buildings hollow at the back,

Streetlights that would topple in a breeze.
Leaving my house, clutching the rubbery basket
I use for farmer's-market vegetables,
Gingerly, I walked into a street

Stripped of actual traffic, to discover
"Freshmen" chattering like orioles. A man
In canvas overalls, crowd choreographer,
Barked syllables in opposite directions,

And set us off, a passersby ballet
Whose paths were planned. Some watched for non-existent
Green lights; one woman nervously
Darted, jostling books from pseudo-students.

Then a flower vendor wheeled a wagon
Past us. An actor ran with outstretched arms,
Missed it and cursed it, green eyes so forlorn
I knew that he would follow those geraniums

Forever. And that was all the cameras
Reeled in that morning: one scene with the same
Brightness that had possessed me over the years
I sailed with Bette Davis in a storm

Of black-and-white, trailed Bogart's enemies
Who wear magenta neckties (colorized),
And wept through *Les Enfants du Paradis*.
When the director let us go, I realized

That the protection of familiar things
Was limited. At best I was a stranger.
Undoubtedly, the market would be traveling
On wheels to another city, and the copy center

Delivered elsewhere, shelves and window panes.
Some crew would sandblast the "U.S. Government
Post Office" block letters, engraved in stone.
Seeing mica glitter on the pavement,

I scrutinized my neighbors for their real
Identities, and warily questioned every
Role. Under the sun's strobe, at my peril,
I staggered into an enamel sky

Knowing my destiny would be geraniums,
Blood-red and quivering on a rickety wagon
I might never encounter, only watch them
Drop velvety petals as they rattled on.

RUSSELL
EDSON

*Making a
Movie*

They're making a movie. But they've got it all wrong. The hero is supposed to be standing triumphantly on the deck of a ship, but instead is standing on a scaffold about to be hanged.

The heroine is supposed to be embracing the hero on the deck of that same ship, but instead is being strapped down for an electric shock treatment.

Crowds of peasants who long for democracy, and are supposed to be celebrating the death of a tyrant are, in fact, carrying that same tyrant on their shoulders, declaring him the savior of the people.

The director doesn't know what's gone wrong. The producer is very upset.

The stunt man keeps asking, now? as he flips and falls on his head.

Meanwhile a herd of elephants stampedes through central casting; and fake flood waters are really flooding the set.

The stunt man asks again, now? and again flips and falls on his head.

The director, scratching his head, says, perhaps the electric shock should be changed to insulin? . . .

Are you sure? asks the producer.

No, but we might as well try it . . . And, by the way, that stunt man's not very good, is he?

COLLEEN J.
MCELROY

*For the Black
Rider of the
Black Hills and
Afternoons of
Saturday
Matinees at the
Antioch
Theatre*

you were pretty
that was your big problem
even your name—Nat Love—
suggested more than you had

if Moran warriors hadn't invented hip-dip walks
to fake their fear in front of lions
you would have claimed that strut as your own
but your first claim was reward posters

where you played for the same stakes as white crooks
horsemen of the Palo Duro called you Desperado
and forgot you were born a slave
Man, you were bad

kid gloves and buckskins tanned jet black
shoulder-length washboard hair, and eyes like knives
you made yourself from the hardest kind of stone
and hillsides quaked at even the sight of you

from Dakota to Mexico you could break stallion or man
end an argument or stampede with a gun
but in the end, it was your story that counted
words more priceless than any posted bond

by 1906, black boys on both sides of the 'ssissippi
knew you as hero of a boundless range
your sly hustler's smile full of cowboy tricks
my daddy left Georgia with your name on his lips
called you Deadwood Dick, bad as what you swore to, Love

Juan, they are still selling you for millions
and me for scenery while I stare too long
at this painter's dream of reality and illusion.
With a face like that of some neighborhood boy
I've loved, you seem caught between a delicate
sense of light and color however unreal,

your smile a scab that has healed
for the moment over some wound
still raw underneath or the master's
choice of venison perhaps,
or some error in paint for the royal dwarf,
a pigment for your Lady's veil,
her throat pulsing at the spur
of the moment on yet another canvas

where you will never sign your name.
But now your only concern is that bitter-
sweet pose of playing the African gallant,
and how to keep your face from growing
too handsome in a country
where courtyards stink of dog shit and mold
and most men have faces like algae.
I would wish you out of that Moorish
kingdom turned Spanish, pull you from
your slave-bound history into my own
where you can take your rein and become
my cavalier with your all-knowing eyes
and urban smile, with your cape spilling
in velvet folds, heartsblood red and waiting.

The Sidney Greenstreet Blues

I think something beautiful
and amusing is gained
by remembering Sidney Greenstreet,
but it is a fragile thing.

The hand picks up a glass.
The eye looks at the glass
and then hand, glass and eye fall away.

LUCILLE
CLIFTON

note, passed to superman

sweet jesus, superman.
if i had seen you
dressed in your blue suit
i would have known you.
maybe that choirboy clark
can stand around
listening to stories
but not you, not with
metropolis to save
and every crook in town
filthy with kryptonite.
lord, man of steel,
i understand the cape,
the leggings, the whole
ball of wax.
you can trust me,
there is no planet stranger
than the one i'm from.

"Since movies were invented we have had no time for description of scenery and for long, drawn-out transitions. Nor for the working out of an obvious plot."

— LOUIS SIMPSON

C. K. WILLIAMS

Nostalgia

In the dumbest movie they can play it on us with a sunrise and a passage of adagio Vivaldi—

all the reason more to love it and to loathe it, this always barely choked-back luscious flood,

this turbulence in breast and breath that indicates a purity residing somewhere in us,

redeeming with its easy access the thousand lapses of memory shed in the most innocuous day

and canceling our rue for all the greater consciousness we didn't have for past, lost presents.

Its illusion is that we'll retain this new, however hammy past more thoroughly than all before,

its reality, that though we know by heart its shabby ruses, know we'll misplace it yet again,

it's what we have, a stage light flickering to flood, chintz and gaud, and we don't care.

MARVIN
BELL

On Location

Blood drips from the eyes of
a woman high in a tree. You can see
this if you get just right on the ground
observing by branch, laddering your look
up the rays of the sun: the crown
she wears who pauses overhead.

Your character wouldn't climb alone
that tree in a movie, the music
telling all who yell to you to hear. But
say you get a chance to be in the film—
a star!—and the Director says "Action!"
looking at you, and everyone motionless.

You might climb, imagining anything.
You could promise yourself big
things, things like being good after
branch three or branch five, where traces
of makeup assert steps to take, and
of course to wash the lipstick off.

DIANE
WAKOSKI

Waiting for the New Tom Cruise Movie: Summer '88

*for Craig who fell over a cliff/
The Fool, in the tarot deck*

83

Try
playing pool
with a sword. Try
remembering
the Navy pilot
who drank clear water.
Try your own
memories
of a world where all the gold
was in somebody else's
safe deposit box,
where you spoke the language
of salamanders
and listened only to *Madame Butterfly*
in English.
                    You see
what you want to see:
The Silver Surfer
out of the comics,
John Rambo, not
Arthur
unless you remember
why he gave up poetry.

And the mind is used
for many purposes:
        "what a relief," says the reviewer,
        "here are poems that do not 'take risks' or
        'break
        new ground' " Oh, Craig,
this lyric is for beautiful young men,
for you,
for Tom Cruise,
for Andrew McCarthy,
and some of the boys who sit in my
eccentric classrooms.

The woman
  who has bandages on her eyes:
  justice?

"O love," he says
"where are you leading me now?" But I know
  where love leads us all.
  To cliffs which, like the fool, we dance willingly
  over. To swamps where the bad girl
  from fairy tales is transformed into a Marsh King's
  daughter.
  To Beethoven's piano, humming and thundering
  in the night or the thirty million dollar
  fighter planes, where you can fly upside-down
  over the enemy before drinking Pepsi,
  to the place where the hoodwinked woman
  stands shivering among crusader swords, and no
  crusaders in sight. To eating an apple
  and becoming Walt Disney's Snow White.

  Love leads us, and we willingly,
  lovingly follow. All our mistakes
  are made for love,
  or greed.
  Love takes more risks
  than greed.

  How can we beguile ourselves?
  Beauty and chaos
  have the same substance,
  look the same from the back;
  which one is dancing ahead,
  leading us,
  never looking back? We turn
  ourselves into coyotes,
  grey and hungry,

and we follow,
running. We
follow without even thinking
it might be
a risk.

DAVID
MELTZER

15th Raga/ For Bela Lugosi

Sir, when you say
Transylvania or wolfbane
or
I am Count Dracula,
your eyes become wide
&, for the moment, pure
white marble.

It is no wonder that
you were so long a junkie.

It's in the smile. The way
you drifted into Victorian bedrooms
holding up your cape like skirts,

then covering her face
as you bent over her to kiss
into her neck & sup.

It is no wonder & it was
in good taste too.

ISHMAEL
REED

Life Is a Screwball Comedy

Life is a screwball comedy
life is a screwball comedy
It's Cary Grant leaning too
far back in a chair
It's Bill Cosby with a
nose full of hair
It's Richard Pryor
with his heart on fire
Life is a screwball comedy
life is a screwball comedy
It's Moms Mabley leaving her
dentures home
It's the adventures of Hope and Bing
It's Bert Williams doin' a buck and wing
It's Stepin Fechit sauntering before
a mule
It's matches in your shoes
It's April Fool
Life is a screwball comedy
Life is a screwball comedy
It's Scatman Crothers with his
sexy grin
It's W. C. Fields with a bottle
of gin
It's Maggie gettin' in her digs
at Jiggs
It's Desi and Lucy having a doozy
of a fight
It's Pigmeat Markham and Slappy White
Life is a Screwball Comedy
Life is a Screwball Comedy
It's Will Rogers twirling a rope
It's Buster Keaton wearing his
famous mope
It's Fatty Arbuckle in a leaking
boat

It's a scared rabbit
And a tricky Coyote
Life is a screwball comedy
Life is a screwball comedy
It's Eddie Murphy's howl
It's Whoopi Goldberg's stroll
It's Fred Allen's jowls
Its Pee-Wee Herman's clothes
It's Hardy giving Laurel a hard time
It's Chaplin up on his toes
Life is a screwball comedy
life is a screwball comedy
life is a screwball comedy
And the joke's on us

CHARLES
SIMIC

Position without a Magnitude

As when someone
You haven't noticed before
Gets up in an empty theater
And projects his shadow
Among the fabulous horsemen
On the screen

And you shudder
As you realize it's only you
On your way
To the blinding sunlight
Of the street.

MICHAEL S.
HARPER

Afterword:
A Film

"grandma's picket fence
balloon mask dancing
bloody moon your
black ribcage."

Erect in the movies
with a new job,
Trader Horn
and *The Gay Woman*
unfold in a twinbill:
drums, wild dancing,
naked men, the silver
veils on the South Side.
He imagines nothing:
it is all before him,
born in a dream:
a gorilla broke loose
from his zoo
in a tuxedo: baboon.
You pick your red bottom.
The Daltons are the movies.

On my wall are pictures:
Jack Johnson, Joe Louis,
Harlow and Rogers:
"see the white god and die."

Underground I live in veils,
brick and cement,
the confession beaten out,
slung with hung carcasses,
a bloody cleaver grunting,
a dead baby in the sewer:
"all the people I saw were guilty."

Marked black I was shot,
double-conscious brother in the veil—
without an image of act or thought
double-conscious brother in the veil—

The rape: "Mrs. Dalton, it's me,
Bigger, I've brought Miss Dalton
home and she's drunk":
to be the idea in these minds,
double-conscious brother in the veil—
father and leader where is my king,
veils of kingship will lead these folks
double-conscious brother in the veil—
"see the white gods and die"
double-conscious brother in the veil—

AL
YOUNG

W. H. Auden &
Mantan
Moreland

*In memory of the
Anglo-American poet & the
Afro-American comic actor
(famed for his role as
Birmingham Brown,
chauffeur in those ancient
Charlie Chan movies) who
died on the same day in 1973*

Consider them both in paradise,
discussing one another—
the one a poet, the other an actor;
interchangeable performers
who finally slipped backstage
of a play whose cast favored lovers.

"You executed some brilliant lines,
Mr. Auden, & doubtless engaged our
innermost emotions & informed imagination,
for I pondered your *Age of Anxiety*
diligently over a juicy order of ribs."
"No shit!" groans Auden, mopping his brow.
"I checked out all your Charlie Chan
flicks & flipped when you turned up again
in *Watermelon Man* & that gas commercial
over TV. Like, where was you all that
time in between? I thought you'd done
died & gone back to England or somethin."

"Wystan, pray tell, why did you ever eliminate
that final line from 'September 1, 1939'?—
We must love one another or die."

"That was easy. We gon die anyway no matter
how much we love, but the best thing I like
that you done was the way you buck them eyes
& make out like you runnin sked all the time.
Now, that's the bottom line of the black
experience where you be in charge of the scene.
For the same reason you probly stopped shufflin."

*Three
Thousand
Hours of
Cinema
by Jean-Luc
Godard*

8 AM
in

2 PM
Terreur

5 PM
for

11 PM
acted

4 PM
which

5 PM
here

11:45 AM
Yet

6 PM
to

10 PM
was

5 PM
her

Noon
they

9 PM
young

5 PM
that

1 AM
Note

3 PM
who

1 PM
best

3 PM
ing

10 AM
me

6 PM
doing

5 PM
bread

2 PM
Barthès

10 PM
pessimistic

STEPHEN
DUNN

An American Film

A rainbow appeared with its promises,
its lore. At a moment like this, I thought,
something might begin for someone else.

The grass was wet. The air chlorophyll.
I walked across the grass
as if I were watching myself

walk across the grass. There was no romance
to the way she waited at the curb
next to the Mazda. She, in fact, was impatient

and I apologized for the lateness
of the hour, the absence
of something graceful, redemptive.

I said, "Look at the rainbow,"
but felt foolish
as if I had said something in song.

Elsewhere things were probably beginning
for other people; kisses, ideas.
We got in the car and drove to Brazil.

No, we got in the car and began
the speaking parts from the life we were in,
then drove to the party.

The sky was a blue helmet
worn by a large invisible clown.
The party was barbecue, backyard.

I knew a good story about a green-head fly
and moved from person to person
telling it. I told it with charm,

hearing myself tell it,
knowing how insignificant it was—
a chance to exhibit pure style.

The woman I arrived with smiled
from across the yard. I felt I should
caress her cheek, take her aside.

Perhaps someone who believed rainbows
were for him, was boarding a plane now
ignorant of the story he was in

as only major characters can be.
The hot dogs smelled like good memories.
The bean salad glistened

on its white tray. It was still afternoon,
still only the middle of what
was not much different

from what it felt like, or seemed.

Picture

Three men on scaffolding scatter corn flakes down
For people to see in black-and-white as snow,
Falling around the actor under the lights.

The actor hunches in the flakes, the set
Is a bitter street, the camera dollies in
And the monster stamps and sorrows, now he's lost,

He shakes his arms and howls, an ugly baby,
Nostrils forced open by little makeup springs.
The dust of corn flakes, trampled underfoot,

Infiltrates his lungs, he starts to wheeze
And so they take a break and start again.
Weeks later, he dies of pneumonia, maybe by chance—

But the picture is finished, people see the scene
And if they know, they feel the extra pathos,
Even if they joke a little about it. The movie

Is silent, corn flakes are a kind of health food,
It's all that long ago, although the picture
Survives as flecks of light and dark on substances

Not invented when they made it—or a play
Of information, a magnetic mist
Of charges, particles too fine to see.

STEPHEN
DOBYNS

What You Have Come to Expect

The worn plush of the seat chafes your bare legs
as you shiver in the air-conditioned dark
watching a man embrace his wife at the edge
of their shadowy lawn. It is just past dusk
and behind them their house rises white and
symmetrical. Candles burn in each window,
while from the open door a blade of light jabs
down the gravel path to a fountain. In the doorway
wait two children dressed for sleep in white gowns.
The man touches his wife's cheek. Although
he must leave, he is frightened for her safety and
the safety of their children. At last he hurries
to where two horses stamp and whinny in harness.
Then, from your seat in the third row, you follow him
through battles and bloodshed and friends lost
until finally he returns home, rides up the lane
as dusk falls to discover all that remains of his house
is a single chimney rising from ashes and mounds of debris.
Where is his young wife? He stares out across
empty fields, the wreckage of stables and barns.
Where are the children who were the comfort of his life?

In a few minutes, you plunge into the brilliant light
of the afternoon sun. Across the street, you see your bike
propped against a wall with your dog waiting beside it.
The dog is so excited to see you she keeps leaping up,
licking your face, while you, still full of the movie,
full of its colors and music and lives sacrificed to some
heroic purpose, try to tell her about this unutterable
sadness you feel on a Saturday afternoon in July, 1950.
Bicycling home, you keep questioning what happened
to the children, what happened to their father standing
by the burned wreckage of his house, and you wish
there were someone to explain this problem to, someone
to help you understand this sense of bereavement and loss:
you, who are too young even to regret the passage of time.

Next year your favorite aunt will die, then your
grandparents, one by one, then even your cousins.
You sit on the seat of your green bike with balloon tires
and watch your dog waiting up the street, a Bayeux
tapestry dog, brindle with thin legs and a greyhound chest—
a dog now no more than a speck of ash in the Michigan dirt.
From a distance of thirty years, you see yourself paused
at the intersection, a thin blond boy in khaki shorts;
see yourself push off into the afternoon sunlight,
clumsily entering your future the way a child urged on
by its frightened nurse might stumble into a plowed field
in the dead of night, half running, half pulled along.
Behind them: gunshots, flame, and the crack of burning wood.
Far ahead: a black line of winter trees.

Now, after thirty years, the trees have come closer.
Glancing around you, you discover you are alone;
raising your hands to your face and beard, you find
you are no longer young, while the only fires
are in the fleck of stars above you, the only face
is the crude outline of the moon's—distant, as any family
you might have had; cold, in a way you have come to expect.

Brownsville Girl

Well, there was this movie I seen one time about a man
Riding 'cross the desert. It starred Gregory Peck. He was shot down
By a hungry kid try'n' to make a name for himself. The towns-people
wanted to crush the kid down and string him up by the neck.

Well the Marshal, now he beat that kid to a bloody pulp
As the dying gunfighter lay in the sun and gasped for his last breath.
Turn him loose, let him go, let him say he outdrew me fair and square,
I want him to feel what it's like to every moment face his death.

Brownsville girl with your Brownsville curls,
Teeth like pearls shining like the moon above.
Brownsville girl, show me all around the world.
Brownsville girl, you're my honey love.

Well I keep seeing this stuff and it just comes a-rolling in
And you know it blows right through me like a ball and chain
You know I can't believe we've lived so long and are still are so far apart
The memory of you keeps callin' after me like a rollin' train.

I can still see the day that you came to me on the painted desert
In your busted down Ford and your platform heels
I could never figure out why you chose that particular place to meet
Ah, but you were right. It was perfect as I got in behind the wheel.

Well we drove that car all night into San Anton'
And we slept near the Alamo, your skin was so tender and soft.
Way down in Mexico you went out to find a doctor and you never came
    back
I would have gone on after you but I didn't feel like letting my head get
    blown off.

Well, we're drivin' this car and the sun is comin' up over the Rockies,
Now I know she ain't you but she's here and she's got that dark rhythm
    in her soul.
But I'm too over the edge and I ain't in the mood anymore to remember
    the times when I was your only man

And she don't want to remind me. She knows this car would go out of
control.

Chorus

Well, we crossed the panhandle and then we headed towards Amarillo
We pulled up where Henry Porter used to live. He owned a wreckin' lot
outside of town about a mile.
Ruby was in the backyard hanging clothes, she had her red hair tied
back. She saw us come rolling up in a trail of dust.
She said, "Henry ain't here but you can come on in, he'll be back in a
little while."

Then she told us how times were tough and about how she was thinkin'
of bummin' a ride back to from where she started.
But ya know, she changed the subject every time money came up.
She said, "Welcome to the land of the living dead." You could tell she
was so broken-hearted.
She said, "Even the swap meets around here are getting pretty corrupt."

"How far are y'all going?" Ruby asked us with a sigh.
"We're going all the way 'til the wheels fall off and burn,
'Til the sun peels the paint and the seat covers fade and the water
moccasin dies."
Ruby just smiled and said, "Ah, you know some babies never learn."

Something about that movie though, well I just can't get it out of my
head
But I can't remember why I was in it or what part I was supposed to
play.
All I remember about it was Gregory Peck and the way people moved
And a lot of them seemed to be lookin' my way.

Chorus

Well, they were looking for somebody with a pompadour,
I was crossin' the street when shots rang out.

I didn't know whether to duck or to run, so I ran.
"We got him cornered in the churchyard," I heard somebody shout.

Well, you saw my picture in the Corpus Christi Tribune. Underneath it,
    it said, "A man with no alibi."
You went out on a limb to testify for me you said I was with you.
Then when I saw you break down in front of the judge and cry real
    tears,
It was the best acting I saw anybody do.

Now I've always been the kind of person that doesn't like to trespass but
    sometimes you just find yourself over the line.
Oh if there's an original thought out there, I could use it right now.
You know, I feel pretty good, but that ain't sayin' much. I could feel a
    whole lot better,
If you were just here by my side to show me how.

Well, I'm standin' in line in the rain to see a movie starring Gregory
    Peck,
Yeah, but you know it's not the one that I had in mind.
He's got a new one out now, I don't even know what it's about
But I'll see him in anything so I'll stand in line.

Chorus

You know, it's funny how things never turn out the way you had 'em
    planned.
The only thing we knew for sure about Henry Porter is that his name
    wasn't Henry Porter.
And you know there was somethin' about you baby that I liked that was
    always too good for this world
Just like you always said there was somethin' about me you liked that I
    left behind in the French Quarter.

Strange how people who suffer together have stronger connections
    than people who are most content.
I don't have any regrets, they can talk about me plenty when I'm gone.

You always said people don't do what they believe in, they just do what's
   most convenient, then they repent.
And I always said, "Hang on to me, baby, and let's hope that the roof
   stays on."

There was a movie I seen one time, I think I sat through it twice.
I don't remember who I was or where I was bound.
All I remember about it was it starred Gregory Peck, he wore a gun and
   he was shot in the back.
Seems like a long time ago, long before the stars were torn down.

Chorus

TOM
CLARK

Final Farewell

Great moment in *Blade Runner* where Roy
Batty is expiring, and talks about how everything
he's seen will die with him—
ships on fire off the shoulder of Orion
sea-beams glittering before the Tannhauser gates.

Memory is like molten gold
    burning its way through the skin
it stops there.
         There is no transfer
Nothing I have seen
will be remembered
beyond me
That merciful cleaning
of the windows of creation
will be an excellent thing
my interests notwithstanding.

But then again I've never been
    near Orion, or the Tannhauser
gates,

I've only been here.

Heroic Simile

When the swordsman fell in Kurosawa's *Seven Samurai*
in the gray rain,
in Cinemascope and the Tokugawa dynasty,
he fell straight as a pine, he fell
as Ajax fell in Homer
in chanted dactyls and the tree was so huge
the woodsman returned for two days
to that lucky place before he was done with the sawing
and on the third day he brought his uncle.

They stacked logs in the resinous air,
hacking the small limbs off,
tying those bundles separately.
The slabs near the root
were quartered and still they were awkwardly large;
the logs from midtree they halved:
ten bundles and four great piles of fragrant wood,
moons and quarter moons and half moons
ridged by the saw's tooth.

The woodsman and the old man his uncle
are standing in midforest
on a floor of pine silt and spring mud.
They have stopped working
because they are tired and because
I have imagined no pack animal
or primitive wagon. They are too canny
to call in neighbors and come home
with a few logs after three days' work.
They are waiting for me to do something
or for the overseer of the Great Lord
to come and arrest them.

How patient they are!
The old man smokes a pipe and spits.
The young man is thinking he would be rich
if he were already rich and had a mule.

Ten days of hauling
and on the seventh day they'll probably
be caught, go home empty-handed
or worse. I don't know
whether they're Japanese or Mycenaean
and there's nothing I can do.
The path from here to that village
is not translated. A hero, dying,
gives off stillness to the air.
A man and a woman walk from the movies
to the house in the silence of separate fidelities.
There are limits to imagination.

SHARON OLDS

The Death of Marilyn Monroe

The ambulance men touched her cold
body, lifted it, heavy as iron,
onto the stretcher, tried to close
the mouth, closed the eyes, tied the
arms to the side, moved a caught
strand of hair, as if it mattered,
saw the shape of her breasts, flattened by
gravity, under the sheet,
carried her, as if it were she,
down the steps.

These men were never the same. They went out
afterwards, as they always did,
for a drink or two, but they could not meet
each other's eyes.

        Their lives took
a turn — one had nightmares, strange
pains, impotence, depression. One did not
like his work, his wife looked
different, his kids. Even death
seemed different to him — a place where she
would be waiting,

and one found himself standing at night
in the doorway to a room of sleep, listening to a
woman breathing, just an ordinary
woman
breathing.

STAN
RICE

*Necking at the
Drive-in Movie*

I'm glad their rouge cream is widening
in the cokebox and their movie
is a liquid camera pupil
like ice cream upstream in a dream
about vulvas.

I'm glad their rash catalogue
is furious with the boygirl
voice of the boy with the brown bowl
haircut that mangles the place
piecemeal with his tiny teeth and his tongue.

I'm glad their shriveled roses
dilate like a fascist fantasy of ants in a fire.
I'm glad they are a Mexico
of parrots melting their crests.
I'm glad their sweet ravings
cream in the gardens of stone.

WILLIAM
MATTHEWS

Sympathetic

In *Throne of Blood,* when they come to kill
Macbeth, the screen goes white. No sound.
It could be that the film has broken,
so some of us look back at the booth,

but it's fog on the screen, and from it,
first in one corner and then in another,
sprigs bristle. The killers close in further—
we're already fogged in by the story—

using pine boughs for camouflage,
and Birnam Forest comes to Dunsinane.
Even in Japanese, tragedy works:
he seems to extrude the arrows

that kill him—he's like a pincushion—,
as if we grew our failures and topples,
as if there were no larger force than will,
as if his life seemed strange to us

until he gave it up, half-king, half-
porcupine. We understand. We too were fooled
by the fog and the pines, and didn't
recognize ourselves, until too late, as killers.

ELLEN BRYANT
VOIGT

*At the Movie:
Virginia, 1956*

This is how it was:
they had their own churches, their own schools,
schoolbuses, football teams, bands and majorettes,
separate restaurants, in all the public places
their own bathrooms, at the doctor's
their own waiting room, in the *Tribune*
a column for their news, in the village
a neighborhood called Sugar Hill,
uneven rows of unresponsive houses
that took the maids back in each afternoon—
in our homes used the designated door,
on Trailways sat in the back, and at the movie
paid at a separate entrance, stayed upstairs.
Saturdays, a double feature drew the local kids
as the town bulged, families surfacing
for groceries, medicine and wine,
the black barber, white clerks in the stores—crowds
lined the sidewalks, swirled through the courthouse yard,
around the stone soldier and the flag,

and still I never *saw* them on the street.
It seemed a chivalric code
laced the milk: you'd try not to look
and they would try to be invisible.
Once, on my way to the creek,
I went without permission to the tenants'
log cabin near the barns, and when Aunt Susie
opened the door, a cave yawned, and beyond her square,
leonine, freckled face, in the hushed interior,
Joe White lumbered up from the table, six unfolding
feet of him, dark as a gun-barrel, his head bent
to clear the chinked rafters, and I caught
the terrifying smell of sweat and grease,
smell of the woodstove, nightjar, straw mattress—

This was rural Piedmont, upper south;
we lived on a farm but not in poverty.
When finally we got our own TV, the evening news
with its hooded figures of the Ku Klux Klan
seemed like another movie—*King Solomon's Mines,*
the serial of Atlantis in the sea.
By then I was thirteen,
and no longer went to movies to see movies.
The downstairs forged its attentions forward,
toward the lit horizon, but leaning a little
to one side or the other, arranging the pairs
that would own the county, stores and farms, everything
but easy passage out of there—
and through my wing-tipped glasses the balcony
took on a sullen glamor: whenever the film
sputtered on the reel, when the music died
and the lights came on, I swiveled my face
up to where they whooped and swore,
to the smoky blue haze and that tribe
of black and brown, licorice, coffee,
taffy, red oak, sweet tea—

wanting to look, not knowing how to see,
I thought it was a special privilege
to enter the side door, climb the stairs
and scan the even rows below—trained bears
in a pit, herded by the stringent rule,
while they were free, lounging above us,
their laughter pelting down on us like trash.

*"I like the movies too. And after all, only
Whitman and Crane and Williams, of the
American poets, are better than the movies."*

— FRANK O'HARA

*"You must have been living a quiet life!
Don't you go to the movies?"*

— T. S. ELIOT

LAUREL
BLOSSOM

Checkpoint

Somebody throws a switch, the klieg lights, it's night
up ahead in the free world, and it's snowing.
Inside the guardhouse there's a Christmas tree on a table,
the tinsel winks to convince me: we're all alike.
This is in Eastern Europe, let's call it
1953, a B movie. Treacherous. I follow procedures, slow
my vehicle to a halt. The guards look as if they're expecting me
to be famous. Or else

they want answers
fast: how long did I stay, what did I think I was doing
in their country, where are the diamonds. I tell them
they have to let me through, my passport is valid. They laugh
at the simple things I believe in, in a language
they think I won't get. I surprise them
by repeating my whole life's story. It takes time.
In the end they're all in love with me, I am famous, I can go
wherever I please, and no hurry, no hurry boys.

In Person: Bette Davis

At the Music Hall
last week, the most varied audience
    ever assembled in Detroit—
    its gay populace émergé,
auto profiteers, idolators from Kalamazoo, shut-ins
blinking from urban and suburban
    TV caves

all came, Bette
(and I could go on listing their fates,
    each $8.50 seat yearning . . .
    for what! two-bit matinees,
the remembered ecstasy of your caustic tongue, the swivelling
cigarette-shaking spitfire
    that is you),

all were on time.
When you entered and said, "What a dump!"
    they shrieked for a wrecking ball
    but you restrained them with love.
They were mike-shy but your fluent witchery again enchanted
again excited to speech all
    wanting grace.

"I can't believe
 ("Yes, it's true, darling"), I can't believe
    I'm talking to Bette Davis!"
     "Bette, which was your *favorite,*
was it Margo Channing or Judith Traherne or Mildred or Jane?"
"They were all such *won*derful roles,
    all of them."

"O Bette, why?
 After so many fabulous parts
    why did you degrade yourself
    and play Baby Jane?" "No, No!

It was a *beau*tiful role, I had a *ball* doing Jane. Remember
I was never a glamour-puss."
   O Bette

You won't autograph
but when a fanatic hurls to the stage
    you proffer your hand; he kisses
    and swoons to the quotidian . . .
Here is erudition scholars would envy: the meek hypothesis,
the forty-year-old rumor; here
    those questions

you have answered
all your life—your co-stars, directors,
    feuds, Oscars, jealousies, kids,
    the *Fortune* poll in '40,
the offer of *Gone With the Wind* passed by (but *Jezebel* remains),
the longing for *Virginia Woolf*
    unfulfilled.

There is nothing
they do not know or will not ask, no film
    they cannot correct you on,
    no secret they have not guessed.
"Bette, why aren't there more tributes for you?" "I don't want tributes,
    when
they see you stumbling to your grave
    they give you

tributes. No thanks!"
Questions persist, no one dares to leave.
    They would gladly use you up
    but when you dismiss, they obey,
each with his or her internal film of you (in black dress and shoes),
the *person* of you at last, and
    forever.

Mentioning James Dean

1

"Who?"

2

Lilacs drifted into my nostrils
like small dirigibles. I brushed
my twelve-year-old haircut carefully.
The impossibility of talking to anyone,
so you mumble, sometimes you whine, but
some things you will outgrow. All of us
have tripped into dark rooms, banging
into still objects, sweating, &
there she was—Mother,
rabbit sounds squirt, come
from inside of your eyes, squinting,
the pain of new light
shredded in thin air.

3

They saw your body in dreams. They saw
it intact, your face blown off or
a clown's, & holding services
they knew you were among them, scrambling
for some sweet love, flesh, or
just a friend's arm, & the swollen
park on Sundays.

4

You took a wrong turn, but
we followed, our eyes nailed
to the bone screen. Take us
back, or let us
feel the seance table
fall apart in our dead fingers.

I R A
S A D O F F

Take One

I am the sheriff lifting
up your dress. You are queen
of the cafés. There isn't a man
in the house who hasn't bought you
a drink. When I wear my white
hat, I fill my mouth with bourbon
and valor. I pretend to be talking
to the bartender. "You ought to be
ashamed of this life," I tell
them all. "What do you want
from me?" you ask. "Nothing
you can give me," I answer.

The silence on the set is for
whichever one of us has forgotten
his lines. The lights go out
forever, someone takes the tables
and chairs, the cameras break
their lenses. Now we are alone,
we are really alone without a word
to say to each other. What
do you want from me you say
again, and again I say nothing
you can give me. So you give me
the nothing you gave everyone
else. We decide to forget what
could have been said, there's nothing
important about this life
we're in, we can always take
another take, we can always take

CAROL
MUSKE

Last Take

I watch them killing my husband.
          Trained assassins, pumping round after
round from behind a camouflage truck:
          they crouch toward his crumpling form.

Under the white floodlights,
          blood jets sputter from his chest,
his head's thrown back. He shouts out a name, sliding down
          the white wall against the damp flag of his shadow.

A little guillotine shuts. Hands sponge the wall.
          He stands, alive again, so there's no
reason to fear this rehearsed fall, his captured cry,
          the badly cast revolution that asked his life.

The damask roses painted on the folding parlor screens
          of the phony embassy are real in a way, but the walls
are fake, and fake, too, the passion of these two naked human bodies
          embracing on the Aubusson: nevertheless, they obsess

the eye like any caress. Off-camera, the actor stroking his stubble
          of beard, the actress's hands on her own small breasts.
Presented with the mirror of our sentiments, it seems
          possible to believe that we love the world, ourselves—

Waiting in the wings like extras, full of desire
          projected away from us. These sky-high fingers
of light imply, off hand, all night we stand in for God here.
          There is nothing to fear, he gets up and falls down again

in slow motion. A boom swings into the frame,
          then out. Loaded dice are shaken onto green felt before
the trembling hands of the unwitting victims. A roulette
          wheel turns: the red, the black, chemin de fer.

The train crosses the border: inside, rows of people jammed
            together, watch, weep. Like Art featuring Life, the real
sky behind the starry backdrop fills with stars. The lovers kiss.
            I want to cry out How much? How much do you love each

other? but the director in his cherry-picker signals another take:
            The sky grows light. It's late.

BRUCE
SMITH

Movies

1. UNIVERSAL PICTURES

I tithe to the darkness and I'm glad
for these dreams the size of a house
painted and painted over the way they are, you could
live in them beautifully, stupidly, pure Plato
and nothing but a single window.

In this one an earth slowly turns away
from Asia and Africa in the midst of a star-clotted Milky Way,
then some music of the spheres and a reassuring
word, in English, appears. After this I will believe anything.

2. I GO SEE *KNIFE IN THE WATER* WITH MY FATHER

We must drive a long way together into the suburbs.
All the people in line look intellectual and work

for firms. I must see this movie
or read a book I have not yet checked out of the library.

My father thinks he knows a man in a neutral
colored sweater. I think I see Heather, a girl

I know from here who let me kiss her
breasts. My father and I sit next to each other

       A poor man is a rich man's fool.

in the dark where a young man puts his hands under

       Ignorant, arrogant, proud, cruel.

a woman's sweater and she just stares

       A rich man has a car and a wife.

back at him and doesn't move. I will not, cannot move

      A poor man knows how to use a knife.

or swallow even when the knife is out and they love

      A poor man loves and disappears.

each other. You don't know if it's the love

      The rich man reappears, fool or murderer.

that makes him tense or the tension that makes him love.

Casting Call

snow in the blood. my lover's coo

the maroon man in the black stingy brim smokes camels
tells me i'm a honorary member of the camera crew
one of the chosen chosen
he hands me a nip of concord grape, paws my thigh
requests my zodiac sign and floor plan
slips me twenty to cover expenses

stars twinkle twinkle in asphalt—one looks down not up

at the unemployment office i await sign-up
for stipend. we've been in a slump since reconstruction
the casting director asks me to strip, looks over
my appointments. tells me my figures don't fill the bill
but he can always use a good secretary

the haitian photographer displays a composite of seductees
at two hundred dinars i can join his line-up
he takes my vital statistics down to ring size
measures my tongue
determines i'm vitamin-M deficient and there's
little hope for cure and less for a part

we don't do black on black

the seersucker film producer doubles as clairvoyant
attempts to decipher my mind-set. decides i'm
just the item he'd like to market. alack it's too late
my kliegs are blown
i'm lost in the parking mall, unable to locate my car
unable to remember my name

on hiatus

James Dean

Night after night,
I danced on dynamite,
as light of foot as Fred Astaire,
until I drove the road
like the back of a black panther,
speckled with the gold
of the cold and distant stars
and the slam, bang, bam
of metal jammed against metal.
My head nearly tore from my neck,
my bones broke in fragments
like half-remembered sentences,
and my body,
as if it had been beaten
by a thousand fists,
bruised dark blue;
yet a breath entered my wide-open mouth
and the odor of sweet grass
filled my nose. I died,
but the cameras kept filming
some guy named James,
kept me stranded among the so-called living,
though if anybody'd let me,
I'd have proved
that I was made of nothing
but one long, sweet kiss
before I wasn't there.

Still, I wear
my red jacket, blue jeans.
Sometimes I'm an empty space in line
at some Broadway cattle call,
or a shadow on a movie screen;
sometimes I caress a woman in her dreams,
kiss, undress her anyplace,
and make love to her

until she cries.
I cry out
as she squeezes me tight
between her thighs,
but when she grabs my hair,
my head comes off in her hands
and I take the grave again.
Maybe I never wanted a woman
as much as that anyway,
or even the spice of man on man
that I encountered once or twice,
the hole where I shoved myself,
framed by an aureole of coarse hair.
By that twilight in '55,
I had devised a way
of living in between
the rules that other people make.
The bongos, the dance classes with Eartha Kitt,
and finally racing cars,
I loved the incongruity of it.
They used to say that I was always on
and couldn't separate myself
from the characters I played,
and if I hadn't died,
I'd have burned out anyway,
but I didn't give Quaker's shit, man,
I gave performances.
I even peed on the set of *Giant*—
that's right—
and turned around
and did a scene with Liz Taylor.
I didn't wash my hands first.
All the same, I didn't need an audience.
That's the difference
between an actor
125   and some sly pretender

who manipulates himself
up on the tarnished silver screen.
I didn't *do* method; I did James Dean.
Since then, the posters, photographs, biographies
keep me unbetrayed by age or fashion,
and as many shows a night as it's requested,
I reenact my passion play
for anyone who's interested,
and when my Porsche
slams into that Ford,
I'm doing one hundred eighty-six thousand
miles a second,
but I never leave the stage.

CHARLIE
SMITH

Character Part

The aging actress makes a salad
in the sink, plunders Boston lettuce
and the dandelion greens, fingers grit
off stalks of celery, accepts the cold water,
the radishes, the purple onion chips,
the tomatoes plump and feverish, the skins
just splitting—*Tomatoed out,* the grocer
said, ripe beyond their time,
but she bought them anyway. She
believes the small work of the world
will save her for a while, believes as best
she can. There are too many memories,
too many nights alone in studios where music
played the strangulations of a fate she ardently
portrayed. Sometimes she became
the character and sensed the snake of
another's life writhing in her legs.
She remembers streets at night,
the sullen, glossy pavement
and the smells of roasted meat, shadows
in a doorway that she passed. A waiter
knew her name, and seemed,
as he arranged the heavy silverware,
to make an altar for her life.
It was quite in the evenings there.
On Mondays she'd drive out to the beach,
never leave the car. Between the dunes
the ocean from a distance seemed undisturbed,
like remains after a struggle's passed. Later,
in her lover's arms, she'd replay the day,
taking parts, being for a while the grass,
then the heaps of petals
underneath the hedgerose banks, the sink of rain
beyond a headland in the West. Like air,

as he labored over her, she'd circulate,
touching down and leaving, praising with her touch
the green flags above the lifeguard stand,
the rocking waters, someone's name written in the sand.

ALBERT
GOLDBARTH

A Film

1.

It's strangely like a man
and a display of toy cars. It is,
in a sense. Collected by the hundred
at the base of the drive-in

movie screen, we're toyed
before the larger life—its anguishes
and joys—that's our life
given grandiosity

of size to match our feelings.
And we come down from the mountains,
down from the keeping of stars,
to watch: a single beam of light

become a world—the oldest story.
Now a woman's joined the man. The second
oldest story is going to start now,
jumbo, with butter, with salt.

2.

The story's thin: some little
aspiration, flawed and baubled.
The dialogue's thin: "I never
thought . . ." "Why, you . . ." A house

is a sheet of cannily painted plywood,
propped by rods. "Inside,"
our days and nights
are taking place on a kind of scale

so enormous, their height and width
must be a function of flattenings like
the cats and dogs receive,
in cartoons, from steamrollers. Maybe

these actors' real lives are convoluted
and fecund . . . All I know is everything,
people, house, a background extending to outer
space, is a coating of white paint.

3.

Out in the mountains around us
tonight, if the paper's correct, a couple
of dozen believers have come to wait
for the end of the world, and their

select ascension—"the Rapture,"
they call it—to some new world.
They have candles. They sing. Their knees
are naked on rock. The date has been

ordained for a decade . . . any minute now,
"the Testament of Fire." And when tomorrow
comes, is snoozy, is crumpled
popcorn boxes like always? Won't their

disappointment be blinding, be the fierce sun
as it rises and covers the lake, covers
it completely, a film
over water that's deep and abiding.

DAVID
LEHMAN

*"Toward a
Definition
of Love"*

1.

Another time they were making love. "It's even better
When you help," she said. That was the second thing
He liked about her: she had memorized hours
Of movie dialogue, as if their life together
In the close apartment, with the street noise,
The crank calls, and the sinister next-door neighbor,
Consisted of roles to be played with panache,
If possible, and with a song in her heart. Was she lying
When she told him she loved him? Or was she
The nude in his bed with her back to him
As if he were a painter in Paris in 1870
And she were a model in Brooklyn in 1992,
And what separated them was a painted ocean
Representing the unbridgeable distance between them,
As between age and youth, Europe and America?
A condition of their romance was its impossibility—
She would have panicked if he had proposed,
Because love was passion consuming itself
Like a flickering cigarette, an ember in an ashtray.

2.

When she went back to sleep, he thought about her
Some more, and what they had done the night before:
Something holy, but with awful consequences,
Like a revolution about to enter its reign of terror.
In the movie, he was the jilted soldier ("don't you still
Love me?") or the Scandinavian philosopher ("he wondered
Why he had to give her up"). But their lines so truly parallel
Though infinite could never meet, and there was no use
Arguing against the despair that had wakened his longing
For her, now that she was gone. There was no way
To make it last, to elaborate a moment of such pleasure,
Sweet and intense, that Faust would have bargained away

His soul for it. In public they acted married. One day
She left. She phoned from the road. A morning of tears
In honor of the first morning he had woken up beside her
With the shades rattling in the window, and the rays
Of light seeping weakly into the room, and the noise
Of the kids playing with a ball in the gutter.

NTOZAKE
SHANGE

*from "mesl
(male english
as a second
language): in
defense of
bilingualism"*

i watch black & white movies the way
    yall hanker after the World Series
not like i'm on first base or nothin
    & i surely won't be pitchin
but i do know how to walk em or
          bring in three wit one hit to the far
outfield

yeah.

i hadda brother & he showed me some things.

but
i learnt what i know bout game-playin
    on saturdays fore dawn on reruns
      of who for you are Jim Brown & Willie Mays/
  when i fly i don't condense to a pigskin
ellipse or a leather suited billiard ball
   popped outta Yankee Stadium
who for you is ecstasy on Wrigley Field
    is Tyrone Power as Zorro
      Ronald Coleman seekin out the
      Guillotine for my honor
not my chastity or my reputation/
   Ronald Coleman's deliberately
  riskin himself cuz/ he loved me so
just on accounta he had offered himself
              to me/
he'd die
  fore that gift was took from me.

STEVEN
BAUER

The Man Who Knew Too Much

Insulted by the rain in Hackettstown,
my stormy father slouches, hands
thrust through his pockets to his thighs.
I pull his sleeve, lean against the brick,
stare at the flashing marquee.
It's a mystery he tells me, kicking
litter in the gutter's gray water.

The boy ahead of me in line
befriends me, squirts me in the eye
from a plastic flower on his lapel.
What's a little extra water?
my father says, and pulls me to his side.

He's so tall the rain gleams
in his hair; his hands are deeply smudged
from newsprint and from oil.
It must be my fault then, his silence,
the way he covers up his hairline with his coat.

Of course the kidnapped son is rescued.
When the lights come up, the floor
around my father is a field of popcorn.
Outside, the rain's intensified, and though
I squint both up and down the sidewalk,
I can't find my friend. All the way home
I wait for the explanation, but the smooth
shush of the wipers tells me Qué
será, será, that's all he has
to say on the subject.

MARK
RUDMAN

Cheyenne

They were shooting *Cheyenne Autumn*
in Cheyenne, not far from the sprinklered suburb
where Eric lived.
Every day we visited the set.
We sat up close, on a gashed and gouged corral gate
which looked too real to be real
in the new Cheyenne.
Eric was misty-eyed with pride.
Cheyenne Autumn was being made in his hometown.
But not in autumn.
John Ford stood on a ladder booming out orders
through a megaphone, the white
actors who played the Indians
gathered around the ladder—the extras
I mean—and the real Indians, some
of them no doubt Cheyenne, were gathered around
the actors; a vocal coach
was running the women and children through
"Shall We Gather at the River."
The white actors weren't idle, even while waiting
they had to rub this darkening cream over
their skin to imitate authentic Indians.
Cheyenne Autumn was wrapped in precious gauze.
John Ford was taking the side of the Indians
after forty years of treating them as devils.
Eric's father flounced down on the couch, pale with weariness,
and told of how he'd treated Sal Mineo's infected toe
as a favor as a relief from cow pokes,
cattle prodders, bronco busters, bar fights . . .
I just can't keep these people from falling.
The actor magic-markered his name across his headshot:
"From Sal Mineo to his *friend*—Eric."
Later, back in Salt Lake, I began to think
about my father's prophecy that I'd return
East at seventeen to seek him out.

That was reason enough not to return.

Then Eric was at the door,
  tossed me a six-pack of Coors.
"When the war is over," he said, "I'll never leave Cheyenne.
"Cheyenne," he said. "You've got to come back."
  I could hear what Eric was thinking
  from the fixed look on his face:
  They're making Cheyenne Autumn, *in autumn, in Cheyenne.*

And the cities were burning.

Be True

Your scrapbook's filled with
pictures of all your leading men
Well, baby, don't put my picture
in there with them
Don't make us some little girl's
dream that can't ever come true
It'd only serve to hurt and make you
cry like you do
Well, baby don't do it to me
and I won't do it to you

You see all the romantic movies
you dream and take the boys home
But when the action fades you're left all alone
You deserve better than this, little girl
can't you see you do?
Do you need somebody to prove it to you?
Well baby, you prove it to me
and I'll prove it to you

Now every night you go out looking for
true love's satisfaction
But in the morning you end up settling for
just lights, lights, lights, lights,
Camera, action, ooh
In another cameo role with some bit player
you're befriending
You're gonna go broken-hearted looking for
that happy ending
Well, girl, you're gonna end up just another
lonely ticket sold
Crying alone in the theatre, as the credits role

You say I'll be like those other guys who
filled your head with pretty lies
And dreams that can never come true
Well, baby, you be true to me and I'll be true to you

DENIS
JOHNSON

Movie within
a Movie

In August the steamy saliva of the streets of the sea
habitation we make our summer in,
the horizonless noons of asphalt,
the deadened strollers and the melting beach,
the lunatic carolers toward daybreak—
they all give fire to my new wife's vision:
she sees me to the bone. In August I disgust her.

And her crazy mixed-up child, who eats with his mouth open
talking senselessly about androids, who comes
to me as I gaze out on the harbor wanting
nothing but peace, and says he hates me,
who draws pages full of gnarled organs and tortured
spirits in an afterworld—
but it is not an afterworld, it is this world—
how I fear them for knowing all about me!

I walk the lanes of this heartless village
with my head down, forsaking permanently
the people of the Town Council, of the ice-cream cone, of the
        out-of-state plate,
and the pink, pig eyes
of the demon of their every folly;
because to say that their faces are troubled,
like mine, is to fail: their faces
are stupid, their faces are berserk, but their faces
are not troubled.
Yet by the Metro
I find a hundred others just like me,
who move across a boiling sunset
to reach the fantastic darkness of a theater
where Paramount Pictures presents
An Officer and a Gentleman.

I am not embarrassed by the tears
streaming over my face as I leave the theater.
I go to the movies as I'd go to the dawn,
and the triumphs there, the things that are brought to light,
the large, sad lives of people not so different
from me, their stories heard
through a tumbler held to the ear
and seen through a gauze of falling sand—
these are my triumphs; I am brought to light.

At home the two of them are asleep.
They can never know who I've been, who I am—
I, an officer and a gentleman, make
some tea and I am not hated.
Now in the famous
movie starring all of us
the themes of an evening commence:
the black gerbils scrape their wheel,
the foghorns call themselves back
out of the fog, the homosexuals
in the quaint hotel sing happy birthday around a piano—
but nothing can disturb my wife and child,
for now they are in another world.

MARK
DOTY

Adonis Theater

It must have seemed the apex of dreams,
the movie palace on Eighth Avenue
with its tiered chrome ticket-booth,
Tibetan, the phantom blonde head

of the cashier floating
in its moon window. They'd outdone each other
all over the neighborhood, raising
these blunt pastiches of anywhere

we couldn't go: a pagoda, a future,
a Nepal. The avenue fed into the entry
with its glass cases of radiant stars,
their eyes dreamy and blown

just beyond human proportions to prepare us
for how enormous they would become inside,
after the fantastic ballroom of the lobby,
when the uniformed usher would show the way

to seats reserved for us in heaven.
I don't know when it closed,
or if it ever shut down entirely,
but sometime—the forties?—

they stopped repainting the frescoes,
and when the plaster fell they merely
swept it away, and allowed
the gaps in the garlands of fruit

that decked the ceiling above the second balcony.
The screen shrunk to a soiled blank
where these smaller films began to unreel,
glorifying not the face but the body.

Or rather, bodies, ecstatic
and undifferentiated as one film ends
and the next begins its brief and awkward exposition
before it reaches the essential

matter of flesh. No one pays much attention
to the screen. The viewers wander
in the steady, generous light washing back
up the long aisles toward the booth.

Perhaps we're hurt by becoming
beautiful in the dark, whether we watch
Douglas Fairbanks escaping from a dreamed,
suavely oriental city—think of those leaps

from the parapet, how he almost flies
from the grasp of whatever would limit him—
or the banal athletics of two or more men who were
and probably remain strangers. Perhaps

there's something cruel in the design
of the exquisite plaster box
built to frame the exotic
and call it desirable. When the show's over,

it is, whether it's the last frame
of Baghdad or the impossibly extended
come shot. And the solitary viewers,
the voyeurs and married men go home,

released from the swinging chrome doors
with their splendid reliefs
of the implements of artistry,
released into the streets as though washed

in something, marked with some temporary tattoo
that will wear away on the train ride home,
before anyone has time to punish them for it.
Something passing, even though the blood,

momentarily, has broken into flower
in the palace of limitless desire—
how could one ever be *done* with a god?
All its illusion conspires,

as it always has, to show us one another
in this light, whether we look to
or away from the screen.

LYNN
EMANUEL

Blond Bombshell

Love is boring and passe, all the old baggage,
the bloody bric-a-brac, the bad, the gothic,
retrograde, obscurantist hum and drum of it
needs to be swept away. So, night after night,
we sit in the dark of the Roxy beside grandmothers
with their shanks tied up in the tourniquets
of rolled stockings and open ourselves like earth
to rain to the blue fire of the movie screen
where love surrenders suddenly to gangsters
and their cuties. There in the narrow,
mote-filled finger of light, she loosens
her dazzling, disciplined torrent of platinum,
like the shaft of a waterfall. She is a blonde
so blond, so blinding, she is a blizzard, a huge
spook, and lights up like the sun the audience
in its galoshes. She bulges like a deuce coupe.
When we see her we say good-bye to Kansas.
She is everything spare and cool and clean,
like a gas station on a dark night or the cold
dependable light of rage coming in on schedule like a bus.

MARIE
HOWE

In the Movies

When a man rapes a woman because he's a soldier and his army's won,
there's always somebody else holding her down, another man,

so the men do it together, or one after the other,
in the way my brothers shot hoops on the driveway with their friends

while we girls watched. Their favorite game was PIG.
A boy had to make the exact shot as the boy before him, or he was a P

I G consecutively until he lost. I've been thinking
about the sorrow of men, and how it's different from the sorrow

of women, although I don't know how—

In the movies, one soldier holds the woman down, his hand over her
    mouth,
and another soldier or two holds down the husband

who's enraged and screaming because he can't help the woman he
    loves.
When the soldiers go, he crawls across the dirt and grass

to reach his wife who's speaking gibberish now.
He kisses her cheek over and over again . . .

—The woman lives on. We see her years later,
answering a man's questions in the drawing room, a crescent scar

just above her lace collar. She's dignified and serene. Maybe
her son has been recently killed, maybe she's successfully

married her daughter. *Then came a difficult time,* she says.
How can a woman love a man? In the movies, a man

rapes a woman because he's a soldier and his army's won, and he
wants to celebrate—all those nights in the dark and the mud—

and there's always someone else holding her down, another soldier, or
a friend, so the men seem to do it together.

EDWARD
HIRSCH

*The Skokie
Theatre*

Twelve years old and lovesick, bumbling
and terrified for the first time in my life,
but strangely hopeful, too, and stunned,
definitely stunned—I wanted to cry,
I almost started to sob when Chris Klein
actually touched me—oh God—below the belt
in the back row of the Skokie Theatre.
Our knees bumped helplessly, our mouths
were glued together like flypaper, our lips
were grinding in a hysterical grimace
while the most handsome man in the world
twitched his hips on the flickering screen
and the girls began to scream in the dark.
I didn't know one thing about the body yet,
about the deep foam filling my bones,
but I wanted to cry out in desolation
when she touched me again, when the lights
flooded on in the crowded theatre
and the other kids started to file
into the narrow aisles, into a lobby
of faded purple splendor, into the last
Saturday in August before she moved away.
I never wanted to move again, but suddenly
we were being lifted toward the sidewalk
in a crush of bodies, blinking, shy,
unprepared for the ringing familiar voices
and the harsh glare of sunlight, the brightness
of an afternoon that left us gripping
each other's hands, trembling and changed.

145

from "Fission"

Now the theater's skylight is opened and noon slides in.
I watch as it overpowers the electric lights,
    whiting the story out one layer further

till it's just a smoldering of whites
    where she sits up, and her stretch of flesh
is just a roiling up of graynesses,
    vague stutterings of
light with motion in them, bits of moving zeros

in the infinite virtuality of light,
    some *likeness* in it but not particulate,
a grave of possible shapes called *likeness*—see it?—something
    scrawling up there that could be skin or daylight or even

the expressway now that he's gotten her to leave with him—
    (it happened rather fast) (do you recall)—

the man up front screaming the President's been shot, waving
    his hat, slamming one hand flat
over the open
    to somehow get
our attention,
in Dallas, behind him the scorcher—whites, grays,
    laying themselves across his face—
him like a beggar in front of us, holding his hat—
    I don't recall what I did,
I don't recall what the right thing to do would be,
    I wanted someone to love. . . .

JIM
CARROLL

Living at the
Movies

for Ted Berrigan

1.

There is a stadium beside my window
                        filled with winter
and it is afternoon   alight and borrowing my tears
so by day the message arrives   and by night
I am writing, marvelous joy of "being sure."
pain sweats the hunger upon its teeth   the days
of white miracles break through   sun over the Harlem River
2:23   the fields are gone, moist and trembling.
she plumbs to the purple earth
                        light rising into her features.

2.

so months of cool flowers close in these arms
decay with their green obscenity. denial of everything
in an instant!
          (how strange to be gone)   (to be sure)
like Rene Magritte devouring an apple
                                    (or two)
that's my language, division of words I know:
                        "love" : "sky"

3.

it is afternoon   a sailor is crying above the waterfall
so we bend our heads and pretend to be praying   yes,
I have abandoned the starlets and their mothers
                        and trees are growing on your avenue,
teeth sweating the hungry pain   takes her away in the form
of death or love and
          O to ease the stupidity of my dreams
in the orange wet of loneliness at midnight
                        where in abandoned towers

a young shepherd is sleeping
(and you know it)

4.

into a swamp this heart is flying
like Mayakovsky's last breath
        death full of gravity and Frank O'Hara
I have abandoned . . . and I am crying   it is midnight
and she knows it. marvelous joy of miracles breaks through
I lick the sweat upon the hungry pain
I wonder if she's ever hungry
                I wonder is she's thinking of pain
it is midnight   she plumbs to the purple day
and O to think of her that way

5.

light rising into our features where
into a swamp this poem is flying the
starlets and their mothers are gone
                        they plumb to the earth extinct

so all that's left is she

                                taken away in the form
                                of death or love
the blue day breaks through in miracles.
the miracles are gone. (how strange to be gone)
like Mayakovsky's last breath.   Rene Magritte
devouring the earth's plumb   light rising into
her features the dark obscenity and O to think
of her that way   it is morning and she is crying
the trees on her avenue are flying   wet orange loneliness
of her stupid dreams disappearing
        into a swamp where rise these purple days.

NICHOLAS
CHRISTOPHER

Film Noir

The girl on the rooftop stares out
over the city and grips a cold revolver.
Laundry flaps around her in the hot night.
Each streetlight haloes a sinister act.
People are trapped in their beds, dreaming of
the A-bomb and hatching get-rich-quick schemes.
Pickpockets and grifters prowl the streets.
Hit-men stalk informers and crooked cops hide in churches.
Are there no more picket fences and tea parties
in America? Does no one have a birthday anymore?
Even the ballgames are fixed, and the quiz shows.
Airplanes full of widows circle the skyline.
Young couples elope in stolen cars.
All the prostitutes were wronged terribly in childhood.
They wear polka dot skirts, black gloves, and trenchcoats.
Men strut around in boxy suits, fedoras, and palm-tree ties.
They jam into nightclubs or brawl in hotel rooms
while saxophone music drowns out their cries.
The girl in the shadows drops the revolver
and pushes through the laundry to the edge of the roof.
Her eyes are glassy, her hair blows wild.
She looks down at her lover sprawled on the sidewalk
and she screams.
A crowd gathers in a pool of neon.
It starts to rain.

"Watching Z in an empty North Dakota theater was one of those small, incremental experiences that fed into personal doubt, the necessary seed of any change or growth. The country in Z seemed terribly foreign, exotic, a large and threatening place—deceptive, dangerous, passionate. As it turned out, it was my first view of the world."

—LOUISE ERDRICH

"Movies are the creation of a new dramatic poetry. Movies offer the richest opportunity since Shakespeare."

—JAMES AGEE

JIMMY SANTIAGO
BACA

Main Character

I went to see
How the West Was Won
at the Sunshine Theater.
Five years old,
deep in a plush seat,
light turned off,
bright screen lit up
with MGM roaring lion—
        in front of me
        a drunk Indian rose,
        cursed
        the western violins
        and hurled his uncapped bagged bottle
        of wine
        at the rocket roaring to the moon.
His dark angry body
convulsed with his obscene gestures
at the screen,
and then ushers escorted him
up the aisle,
and as he staggered past me,
I heard his grieving sobs.
        Red wine streaked
        blue sky and take-off smoke,
        sizzled cowboys' campfires,
        dripped down barbwire,

        slogged the brave, daring scouts
        who galloped off to mesa buttes
        to speak peace with Apaches,
        and made the prairie
        lush with wine streams.
When the movie
was over,
I squinted at the bright
sunny street outside,
looking for the main character.

*from
"Pasolini"*

2 NINETTO AT EVENING

While he was preparing The Gospel, *Pasolini discovered the teen-age
Ninetto Davoli in the Roman slums . . .*

Last night, drunk, weaving home from the café,
I stumbled, and this punk hauled me in his arms,
a Madonna of sorts, and we crashed through
the doorway, across the table, glasses
splintering on the floor, chicken bones
and a greasy stain. I asked him if he loves me.
Silence. And then laughter rocked his body,
and suddenly I was grinning too, a harlequin
gulping on a wine bottle, red slivers
running down my lips. He put on a record
and began to dance . . .

A natural actor, Ninetto played in most of Pasolini's films from The
Gospel *on.*

                         Later he shoved me
down like a drowning girl, and the bristles
of his beard brushed my spine, and his fingers
slipped through my sphincter's flower, formed
a fist which ground me open, dug for organs
hidden like diamonds. Feeling myself pound,
twist and plead, jammed round his wrists, I
stared past the boundary where beauty starts—

Though he later married, Ninetto was, for a time, Pasolini's lover.

(So I, turning my head in the gap,
like a screw driven from my mother into
the world, burst out, soundly and beautifully,
horrifed and blue)—

Despite his passion for Ninetto, his nightly forays continued.

>   . . . After he left I kissed
> the ghost of his body in the wrinkled whiteness.

And sometimes, in Rome and in Africa, his friends found him beaten,
*   bleeding.*

ANA
CASTILLO

Seduced by Natassja Kinski

I always had a thing for Natassja Kinski.
My Sorbonne clique and I went to see her latest film. Giant
billboards all over Paris: Natassja—legs spread, her
lover's face lost between.

I watched *Paris, Texas* twice, living with
the eternal memory of those lips
biting into a fleshy strawberry in Tess.
Thank you, Roman Polanski.

Long after I have gotten over Natassja Kinski,
I am with a Chicago clique on holiday. I am an atom now,
in constant, ungraspable flux, when my Bulgarian scarf is
pulled off my neck. It is Natassja Kinski.

She has removed her KGB black-leather coat; bottom of
the ocean eyes are working me, and yes, that mouth . . .

When we dance, I avoid her gaze.
I am trying every possible way to escape eyes,
mouth, smile, determination, scarf pulling me
closer, cheap wine, strobe light, dinner invitation,
"Come home with me. It's for fun," she says.

I dance with her friends again. I am a tourist in my
hometown, and the girls are showing me a good time.
I think *I'll leave with someone else.*
But she finds me at a table in the dark.
"What do you want, my money?" I ask. She reminds, cockily,
that she has more money than I do. I am a poet, everybody
does. And when we dance, I am a strawberry, ripened and
bursting, devoured, and she has won.

We assure each other, the next day, neither of us has
ever done anything like that before.

By Sunday night, we don't go out for dinner as planned.
Instead, over a bottle of champagne,
Natassja wants me forever. Unable to bear that mouth,
sulking, too sad for words, I whisper: *"te llevaré conmigo."*
As if I ever had a choice.

DAVID TRINIDAD

Things to Do in Valley of the Dolls (The Movie)

Move to New York.
Lose you virginity.
Become a star.
Send money to your mother.

Call pills "dolls."
Fire the talented newcomer.
Have a nervous breakdown.
Suffer from an incurable degenerative disease.

Sing the theme song.
Do your first nude scene.
Wear gowns designed by Travilla.
Become addicted to booze and dope.

Scream "Who needs you!"
Stagger around in a half-slip and bra.
Come to in a sleazy hotel room.
Say "I am merely traveling incognito."

Get drummed out of Hollywood.
Come crawling back to Broadway.
Pull off Susan Hayward's wig
and try to flush it down the toilet.

End up in a sanitarium.
Hiss "It wasn't a nuthouse!"
Get an abortion.
Go on a binge.

Detect a lump in your breast.
Commit suicide.
Make a comeback.
Overact.

The Most Beautiful Blonde in the World

All day long she's been appearing.
Visions of Marilyn Monroe
during brunch, at tea
and for my midnight snack.

Waiters hand me her autograph.
Clerks throw in the nude calendar spread
along with my buttons.
Is it possible that she is seeking me out?
And just when I was beginning to lose interest.

Marilyn in blue bathing suit
tugging a rope that rings a little bell
somewhere in heaven where I am
walking on clouds.

Her initials are M & M,
melts in your mouth
and mine are E E,
easily entertained.
Together that spells me.

Me, as in, "If you still want me, I'm all yours!"
Yes, she really said that.
And I told her, I;d think it over.

TINO
VILLANUEVA

The 8 O'Clock
Movie

Boston, 1973 — Years had passed and I assumed a
Different life when one night, while resting from
Books on Marlborough Street (where things like
This can happen), there came into my room images

In black-and-white with a flow of light that
Would not die. It all came back to me in different
Terms: characters were born again, met up with
Each other in adult life, drifted across the

Screen to discover cattle and oil, travelled miles
On horseback in dust and heat, characters whose
Names emerged as if they mattered in a history
Book. Some were swept up by power and prejudice

Toward neighbors different from themselves,
Because that is what the picture is about, with
Class distinctions moving the plot along. A few
Could distinguish right from wrong; those who

Could not you condemned from the beginning when
You noticed them at all. Still others married or
Backed off from the ranch with poignant flair,
Like James Dean, who in the middle of grazing land

Unearthed the treasures of oil, buried his soul in
Money and went incoherent with alcohol. When the '40s
Came, two young men were drafted, the one called *Angel*
Dying at war. It's a generational tale, so everybody

Aged once more and said what they had to say along the
Way according to the script. And then the end: the
Hamburger joint brought into existence to the beat of
"The Yellow Rose of Texas," Juana and her child the

Color of dark amber, foreshadowing the Mexican-looking
Couple and their daughter, all in muteness, wanting
To be served. I climbed out of bed and in my head
Was a roaring of light—words spoken and unspoken

Had brought the obliterated back. Not again (I said,
From my second-floor room) . . . let this not be happening.
Three-and-a-half hours had flicked by. As the sound
Trailed off into nothing, memory would not dissolve.

LOUISE
ERDRICH

Dear John Wayne

August and the drive-in picture is packed.
We lounge on the hood of the Pontiac
surrounded by the slow-burning spirals they sell
at the window, to vanquish the hordes of mosquitoes.
Nothing works. They break through the smoke screen for blood.

Always the lookout spots the Indians first,
spread north to south, barring progress.
The Sioux or some other Plains bunch
in spectacular columns, ICBM missiles,
feathers bristling in the meaningful sunset.

The drum breaks. There will be no parlance.
Only the arrows whining, a death-cloud of nerves
swarming down on the settlers
who die beautifully, tumbling like dust weeds
into the history that brought us all here
together: this wide screen beneath the sign of the bear.

The sky fills, acres of blue squint and eye
that the crowd cheers. His face moves over us,
a thick cloud of vengeance, pitted
like the land that was once flesh. Each rut,
each scar makes a promise: *It is
not over, this fight, not as long as you resist.*

Everything we see belongs to us.

A few laughing Indians fall over the hood
slipping in the hot spilled butter.
The eye sees a lot, John, but the heart is so blind.
Death makes us owners of nothing.
He smiles, a horizon of teeth
the credits reel over, and then the white fields

again blowing in the true-to-life dark.
The dark films over everything.
We get into the car
scratching our mosquito bites, speechless and small
as people are when the movie is done.
We are back in our skins.

How can we help but keep hearing his voice,
the flip side of the sound track, still playing:
Come on, boys, we got them
where we want them, drunk, running.
They'll give us what we want, what we need.
Even his disease was the idea of taking everything.
Those cells, burning, doubling, splitting out of their skins.

MICHAEL
WARR

Die Again Black Hero: Version II

Chicago
March 1990

Predictable.
So same-old-shit predictable.
The Marine whose skin
Matches the surface color
Of an Uzi has to die first.
Even on another planet
This dogma cannot be escaped.
The obsidian one, the last one in line,
Has to be sacrificed to save the other.
It's ingrained in the plot—
Written for "Birth of a Nation"
And repeated ad nauseam.
These men. These scripted, imagined men,
Are either supermen or disabled men
Who cannot be whole.
If computer prodigies
They are confined
To intelligent wheelchairs,
Brilliant, crippled, vulnerable
And prepared to die.
Their lovers are
Data-simulated replicants,
Human relationships are denied them.
Normality is an anomaly for them.
Tailored oddity nourishes their isolation
Their demise inconsequential
Existing to serve, entertain and protect.
As half-men, men with parts missing,
They are less threatening—
In their presence other men
Glow in an aura of superiority
So we will not know
We are all meant
To remain inferior.

THYLIAS
MOSS

Hattie and the Power of Biscuits

This one is about dignity, they all
are. Hattie was an awful big
maid. Her cannon shape was appropriate
for what came out of her. She
gave context to *Gone With the Wind*, she
is what outlived Tara in significance.

In 1939 she received her Oscar for
the best supporting role, the best job
holding up the confederacy, nourishing the
nation, the white family she was *like* a
member of without being trucked into a goose-
down bed or appearing in the albums brought out
on holidays. Hers was the power of biscuits.
What a wonder she didn't use strychnine dough.
Hers was the power of the backdoor key, the
privilege to see how they really live. What
a way to start believing in yourself, to know
you don't ever want to be white. Hattie had
her bones dyed.

Biscuits cut from her cheeks by household
pinches that today reset circuit breakers in
overloaded homes. She worked so hard
the effort churned her salty milk, babies
raised on cheesiness and butter, able to siphon
anything through a straw.

PATRICIA
SMITH

*Why I Like
Movies*

for Charlotte

1.

I like movies because
people get to mug their faces in movies
or walk around with bad posture
and no one yells
"Stop that mugging" or "Stand up straight!"

2.

I like movies because
faces become monuments to promise.

3.

I like movies because
they spark nationalistic conversations
such as
"I never go to French movies, they're
 so pretentious and intellectual."
 or
"Italians must be terribly affected by sex.
 Just think of those voluptuous women, always
 waiting. Anna Magnani, what a face!"
 or
"There's nothing like an American movie musical.
 All that razzle dazzle disguising the petit anguish
 beneath the smiles. Blah, blah, blah."

4.

I like movies because
they say a lot about the Other.
Like Black Folks in America. Those natives in Tarzan
movies with processes and straightened hair. That buffoon
rolling his eyes towards the coming thunder or talking

casually to spooks, saints and children. The women who
tended the house of the seemingly rich with gestures meant
for either tenderness or reproach. Secrets studded in
their enormous flesh.

5.

I like movies because
I never saw myself in them.
I saw the dreams of a people
who looked like spooks, saints
and acted like children.

6.

I like movies because
as the last reel winds back upon itself:
image on image
time turns away
a revolution terrified of the dark.

JASON
SHINDER

Dark Palace

Gables Theater,
Merrick, New York

1

A little dark is all it takes.

And then your eyes.

I can talk out loud,
follow you anywhere, look up
at the ceiling,

but I can't find the strength
to touch you . . .

2

I hold fear over everything,
sea, moon, stars,

the few essential images
in which I almost believe.

3

It used to be I saw you
every so often.

Now every evening I go out
to see what kind of dark it is.

Do not mistake me.

Nothing is clear.

I expect a stone
to open an old sorrow.

4

The moon assails a window
where your bare back
is all I see.

I am not ashamed
to raise my fists
in want of you.

It is only the wind
on your face;
God's breath, God's rough cheek,
that stops me from trembling.

5

I must have lied.

I must have passed the green
of my neighbor's Spruce

once too often
without stopping,

so that what I know
can no longer be sustained.

6

Why isn't your blond hair
beside me?

Is nothing real,

even the diamond
pressed in your hand?

7

I listen to the beating of drums,
enormous stones clashing,
that mouth of yours, those lips.

What was it you said?

I'll go crazy trying to remember.

L U C I E
B R O C K - B R O I D O

So Long, I've Had You Fame

How odd that she would die into an August
night, I would have thought
she would have gone out in a pale clear
night of autumn, covered to the shoulder
in an ivory sheet, hair
fanned out across the pillow perfectly.
Fame will go by, and, so long, I've had you, Fame.
From under the door, the lights leak
into the hall & Sinatra going
over & over in the bedroom on repeat.
I was six & you were dying out.
I was sitting in a sky blue metal chair
in our kitchen in the east
digesting the fact, still, of my mother's second
honeymoon & the man living all over
our house, that she loved him, had him hard.
The sun was on our kitchen table, lighting
the back of my hand & the headline
in the *Post Gazette* said you were done.
That you were dying
even in the hour when our neighborhood
went indigo last night, in the hour
when our palms were stained by Sno-Cones,
in the hour when Russell's father would take home
the bases from the baseball diamond,
then my sister & I would move like spiders
into the nests of our dotted swiss nightgowns,
in the hours of a windless August night
in Pittsburgh & somewhere
Sinatra redundant
no one lifts the needle up, he's singing
like an angel
all night long along the famous dusk
of the Pacific shoreline

as your breathing slowed into the sweetest
toxic nothingness, so long, I've had you, face
down,   *Cursum Perficio.*

DIONISIO D. MARTINEZ

Reenactments

—for Rosa Menéndez

Cinéma vérité, she says, as if that
were enough to convince us.

The girl at the car rental agency has that Jean Harlow
look about her. On my way to Kentucky at two
in the morning I begin to drive backward through time,
my future dissolving in the rearview mirror.

She changes her name to protect her innocence.

At the novelty store someone is buying a poster of
Patty Hearst playing Tania: armed with the look
of someone whose weapon is loaded. Behind her a cobra
is about to strike. Resemblances between Tania
and the reptile have gone unnoticed, unexamined.
When the customer begins to roll up the poster,
the cashier says, "I saw that movie too."

She believes in degrees of perfection—
with each successive frame the subject
is closer and larger yet somehow less defined.

A revival house in Buenos Aires is showing *Blow Up*
to an audience consisting solely of Julio Cortázar,
who has been dead for years and sits in the front
row, wringing his hands in frustration: he has trouble
picking up and connecting the clues.
It appears he's distracted by a premonition.

Art imitates art, she says. It's the nature
of things.

A M Y
GERSTLER

Slowly I Open My Eyes

(gangster soliloquy)

While the city sleeps there's this blast of silence that follows the whine of daylight: a defeat that wraps itself around buildings like a python, or one of those blue sheets they bundle corpses up in. *Wanna go for an ambulance ride?* Fragments of the sordid and the quote unquote normal vie for my attention. Hacking coughs and seductive yoo-hoos dangle in the 3 A.M. air. Up on this roof, I smoke cigarettes and wait. I feel like god up here. No kidding. Jerusalem Slim on his final night in the garden. Mr. X., Dr. No., The Invisible Man. All the same guy, different movies. It's a city of delinquents: my disciples. Maybe some bum down below finds one of my stubbed out butts and is delighted. Everybody's looking for something to inhale and something else to empty into. The whole city reels and twinkles at my feet, but the stars aren't impressed. They see it every night. The eighty-year-old elevator operator downstairs snores like he's trying to suck up the Hudson. Humans act as if they're going to stick around forever, but nobody ever does. That's what cracks me up.

LEWIS
BUZBEE

Sunday, Tarzan in His Hammock

When the king of the jungle first wakes up, he thinks
it's going to be a great day, as laden with possibility
as the banana tree with banana hands, but by ten
he's still in the hammock, arms and legs dull as
termite mounds. He stares at the thatched roof and realizes
that his early good mood was a leftover from Saturday,
when he got so much done: a great day, he saved
the tiger cub trapped in the banyan, herded the hippos
away from the tourists and their cameras and guns,
restrung and greased the NNW vines, and all by noon.
All day he went about his duties, not so much kingly duties
as custodial, and last night, he and Cheetah went for a walk
under the ostrich-egg moon. This morning nothing stirs him.
The world is a stagnant river, a scummy creek's dammed pool.
Cheetah's gone chattering off, Jane is in town,
and the rest of the animals are busy with one another—
fighting, eating, mating. Tarzan can barely move,
he does not want to move. Does the gazelle ever feel this
lassitude, does it ever want to lie down and just stare,
no longer caring for its own safety, tired of the vigilance?
Does the lion, fat in the grass, ever think, fuck it,
let the wounded springbok live, who cares?
Tarzan thinks maybe he'll go to the bathing pools
and watch the village girls bathe, splashing in the sun,
their breasts and thighs perfect. He wishes someone would
bring him a gourd of palm wine, a platter
of imported fruits—kiwi, jackfruit, star fruit—
or maybe a bowl of roasted yams slathered in goat butter,
maybe Jane will bring him a book. Nothing will be delivered.
He hears far off in the dense canopy a zebra's cry for help,
those damned jackals again, but, no, he will not move.
Let the world take care of itself, let the world eat
the world. He can live without the call of the wild.
He thinks.

DIANN
BLAKELY
SHOAF

Reunion Banquet, Class of '79

"What happened to Charlotte Rampling?"—the vamp
and villainess of freshman year's remake,
Farewell, My Lovely. I can't recall the plot,
nor which boyfriend I went to see it with,

none villains. Freshman year, girls learn to drink;
we spent weekends bombed in years that followed,
often with those old boyfriends, some seated
in nearby chairs as we discuss *Three Women, Klute*

("poor Sutherland—what was the bomb that followed?"
"Fellini's *Casanova*"; Jane Fonda
changing women from fat dateless klutzes
to lean wives, marrying "that Turner guy,

a fellow Casanova before Jane.")
Chinatown, Looking for Mr. Goodbar;
Diane Keaton ferrying from guy to guy
then killed. *Helter Skelter,* a TV movie

looked at with Chinese food and tepid beer,
that crammed dorm room (soph year? junior?), our knees
jellied. Hell, what's better than the movies
for filling gaps, for steering talk away

from this crammed corner's melodramas, its queens
of bad luck? Emma's three miscarriages—
"children fill a gap"; talk tries to veer away
but she tells us about her absent husband,

who blames their bad luck on her mom's DES,
how she spends Saturday nights now, fevered
by secrets she doesn't tell her husband:
chlamydia and one nostril scarred from coke,

for instance. *Saturday Night Fever!*
someone yelps, and Nan's atop the table—
clam sauce spotting her skirt, a Diet Coke
spilled in the famous John Travolta pose;

someone yelps as Nan tips from the table,
as Layne prescribes a single mom's sanity;
sitcom repeats, like the John Travolta show
about the teacher, while she plugs into

tapes that prescribe ways to keep your sanity
while raising a small boy alone. Virginia
weeps—loudly—about the teacher who plugged her
senior year, and the men at the next table

rise to leave. "So long, boys," and the "virgins,"
sneers Laura, meaning none have been divorced,
not since senior year, when one at their table
tied the knot and wanted out weeks later.

The Deer Hunter. Most seated here are divorced,
and childless too. *Lipstick. Who'll Stop the Rain?*
I untie my knotted napkin, wanting out. It's late.
Woman Under the Influence. Badlands.

"What happened to our apple charlottes?" Vanished,
like our lipsticked smiles, the bottles of wine.
We're women fluent with address pads and pens:
farewell, my lovelies. "I'll call, or write."

ELISE
PASCHEN

Red Lanterns

*"Where the master spends the
night that mistress gets . . .
the lighted lanterns."*

(*Second mistress to
fourth mistress in* Raise the
Red Lantern)

I have seen black-robed men
hang the adultress,
take her, with tied wrists, ankles,
tangled hair, choked entreaties,
across a snow-bound roof
before the household wakes.

I have wound up the gramophone,
played her voice singing,
filled my room with red light,
unbraided my hair, walked
the chambers, expecting the master,
wanting his son.

I have faked pregnancies,
abused the serving girl
(the master's favorite), revealed
secrets in the heat of drink,
refused his kisses,
the solicitude of the women.

In each woman's courtyard
I will raise the red lantern.

TOM
ANDREWS

Cinema Vérité: The River of Barns

Wide-angle shot of a large river swollen with barns of all sizes, in various stages of disintegration. Dusk. Crickets. A man and woman walk by.

Man: How'd all those barns get in the river?
Woman: Beats me.

They watch the barns float and bob in the current for a while, then walk away. Fireflies flicker in the grass.

Permissions

Ai: "James Dean" is from *Fate*. Copyright © 1991 by Ai. Reprinted by permission of Houghton Mifflin Company.

Andrews, Tom: "Cinema Vérité: The River of Barns" is used by permission of the author.

Angelou, Maya: "Miss Scarlett, Mr. Rhett and Other Latter-Day Saints" is from *The Complete Collected Poems of Maya Angelou* (New York: Random House, 1994). Copyright © 1969 by Hirt Music Inc. Reprinted by permission of Hirt Music Inc., c/o Gerard Purcell Associates, Inc.

Ashbery, John: "Farm Film" is from *Shadow Train* (New York: Viking Penguin, 1981). Copyright © 1981 John Ashbery. Reprinted by permission of Georges Borchardt, Inc. for the author.

Baca, Jimmy Santiago: "Main Character" is from *Black Mesa Poems*. Copyright © 1986, 1987, 1988, 1989 by Jimmy Santiago Baca. Reprinted by permission of New Directions Publishing Corporation.

Baraka, Amiri: "Jim Brown on the Screen" is from *Selected Poems*. Copyright © 1975 by Amiri Baraka. Reprinted by permission of Sterling Lord Literistic.

Bauer, Steven: "The Man Who Knew Too Much" is from *Daylight Savings* (Layton, Utah: Gibbs Smith, 1989). Copyright © 1989 by Steven Bauer. Reprinted by permission of the author.

Belitt, Ben: "Soundstage" is from *Possessions* (Boston: David R. Godine, 1986). Copyright © 1964 by Ben Belitt. Reprinted by permission of the author.

Bell, Marvin: "On Location" is from *Iris of Creation*. Copyright © 1990 by Marvin Bell. Reprinted by permission of the author and Copper Canyon Press, PO Box 271, Port Townsend, WA 98368.

Berrigan, Ted: "XXXVIII" is from *The Sonnets* (New York: Grove Press, 1964). Copyright © 1994 by Alice Notley, executor of the Estate of Ted Berrigan. Reprinted by permission of Viking Penguin, a division of Penguin Books USA, Inc.

Berryman, John: "Homage to Film" is from *John Berryman Collected Poems, 1937–1971*, edited by Charles Thornbury. Originally published in the *Southern Review 4* (spring 1940) Copyright © 1940 and renewed © 1968 by John Berryman. Reprinted by permission of Kate Donahue. Reprinted by permission of Farrar, Straus & Giroux, Inc.

Blossom, Laurel: "Checkpoint" is from *What's Wrong*. Copyright © 1987 by Laurel Blossom. Reprinted by permission of author.

Brautigan, Richard: "The Sidney Greenstreet Blues" is from *The Pill Versus the Springhill Mine Disaster*. Copyright © 1989 by Richard Brautigan. Reprinted by permission of Ianthe Brautigan Swenson.

Brock-Broido, Lucie: "So Long, I've Had You Fame" is from *A Hunger*. Copyright © 1988 by Lucie Brock-Broido. Reprinted by permission of the author and Alfred A. Knopf, Inc.

Buzbee, Lewis: "Sunday, Tarzan in His Hammock" is used by permission of the author.

Carroll, Jim: "Living at the Movies" is from *Living at the Movies*. Copyright © 1969, 1971, 1973 by Jim Carroll. Reprinted by permission of Viking Penguin, a division of Penguin Books USA, Inc.

Carroll, Paul: "Ode to Fellini on Interviewing Actors for a Forthcoming Film" is from *Odes* (Big Table Publishing, 1969). Copyright © 1969 by Paul Carroll. Reprinted by permission of the author.

Castillo, Ana: "Seduced by Natassja Kinski" is reprinted by permission of the author.

Christopher, Nicholas: "Film Noir" is from *A Short History of the Island of Butterflies.* Copyright © 1986 by Nicholas Christopher. Reprinted by permission of Viking Penguin, a division of Penguin Books USA, Inc.

Clampitt, Amy: "*The Godfather* Returns to Color TV" is from *What the Light Was Like.* Copyright © 1985 by Amy Clampitt. Reprinted by permission of Alfred A. Knopf, Inc.

Clark, Tom: "Final Farewell" is from *Sleepwalker's Fate: New and Selected Poems, 1965–1991* (Santa Rosa, California: Black Sparrow, 1992). Copyright © 1987 by Tom Clark. Reprinted by permission of the author.

Clifton, Lucille: "note, passed to superman" is from *The Book of Light.* Copyright © 1993 by Lucille Clifton. Reprinted by permission of Copper Canyon Press, P. O. Box 271, Port Townsend, WA 98368.

Coleman, Wanda: "Casting Call" is from *Heavy Daughter Blues: Poems & Stories 1968–1986.* Copyright © 1987 by Wanda Coleman. Reprinted by permission of Black Sparrow Press.

Coolidge, Clark: "Three Thousand Hours of Cinema by Jean-Luc Godard" is used by permission of the author.

Cooper, Jane: "Seventeen Questions about King Kong" is from *The Green Notebook, Winter Road.* Copyright © 1994 by Jane Cooper. Reprinted by permission of the author and Tilbury House, Publishers, Gardiner, Maine.

Corso, Gregory: "Errol Flynn—On His Death" is from *Mindfield: New and Selected Poems.* Copyright © 1989 by Gregory Corso. Reprinted by permission of Thunder's Mouth Press.

Crane, Hart: "Chaplinesque" is from *Complete Poems of Hart Crane,* edited by Marc Simon. Copyright 1933, © 1958, 1966 by Liveright Publishing Corporation. Copyright © 1986 by Marc Simon. Reprinted by permission of Liveright Publishing Corporation.

Creeley, Robert: "The Movie Run Backward" is from *The Collected Poems of Robert Creeley 1945–1975.* Copyright © 1983 by the Regents of the University of California. Reprinted by permission of of the Regents of the University of California, the University of California Press, and the author.

cummings, e. e.: "death is more than" is from *Complete Poems 1904–1962,* edited by George J. Firmage. Copyright © 1926, 1954, © 1991 by the Trustees for the E. E. Cummings Trust. Copyright © 1985 by George James Firmage. Reprinted by permission of Liveright Publishing Corporation.

Dobyns, Stephen: "What You Have Come to Expect" is from *Black Dog, Red Dog,* Copyright © 1980, 1982, 1983, 1984 by Stephen Dobyns. Reprinted by permission of Holt Rinehart & Winston, Inc.

Doty, Mark: "Adonis Theater" is from *Bethlehem in Broad Daylight* (Boston: David R. Godine, 1991). Copyright © 1991 by Mark Doty. Reprinted by permission of the author.

Dugan, Alan: "Homo Ludens: On an Argument with an Actor" is from *New and Collected Poems: 1961–1983.* Copyright © 1983 by Alan Dugan. Reprinted by permission of The Ecco Press.

Duncan, Robert: "Ingmar Bergman's *Seventh Seal*" is from *The Opening of the Field.*

Goodman, Paul: "A Documentary Film of Churchill" is from *Collected Poems*, edited by Taylor Stoehr. Copyright © 1973 by Paul Goodman. Reprinted by permission of Random House, Inc.

Graham, Jorie: The excerpt from "Fission" is from *Region of Unlikeliness*. Copyright © 1991 by Jorie Graham. Reprinted by permission of The Ecco Press.

Guest, Barbara: The excerpt from "Motion Pictures" is used by permission of the author.

Harper, Michael S.: "Afterword: A Film" is from *Images of Kin: New and Selected Poems* published by the University of Illinois Press. Copyright © 1984 by Michael S. Harper. Reprinted by permission of the author.

Hass, Robert: "Heroic Simile" is from *Praise*. Copyright © 1974, 1975, 1976, 1977, 1978, 1979 by Robert Hass. First published by The Ecco Press in 1979. Reprinted by permission.

Hayden, Robert: "Double Feature" is from *Collected Poems of Robert Hayden*, edited by Frederick Glaysher. Copyright © 1982 by Irma Hayden. Reprinted by permission of Liveright Publishing Corporation.

Hirsch, Edward: "The Skokie Theatre" is from *Wild Gratitude*. Copyright © 1985 by Edward Hirsch. Reprinted by permission of Alfred A. Knopf, Inc.

Hollander, John: "The Movie" is from *Blue Wine and Other Poems*. Copyright © 1979 by John Hollander. Reprinted by permission of the Johns Hopkins University Press.

Howe, Marie: "In the Movies" is used by permission of the author.

Hughes, Langston: "Movies" is from *Collected Poems*. Copyright 1994 by the Estate of Langston Hughes. Reprinted by permission of Alfred A. Knopf, Inc.

Jarrell, Randall: The excerpt from "The Lost World" is from *The Complete Poems*. Copyright © 1949, 1969 by Mrs. Randall Jarrell. Reprinted by permission of Farrar, Straus & Giroux, Inc.

Johnson, Denis: "Movie within a Movie" is from *The Veil*. Copyright © 1987 by Denis Johnson. Reprinted by permission of Alfred A. Knopf, Inc.

Kees, Weldon: "Subtitle" is from *The Collected Poems of Weldon Kees*, edited by Donald Justice. Copyright © 1975 by the University of Nebraska Press. Reprinted by permission of University of Nebraska Press.

Kerouac, Jack: "To Harpo Marx" is from *Poems All Sizes* (Pocket Series #48). Copyright © 1959 by Jack Kerouac. Reprinted by permission of City Lights Books.

Kunitz, Stanley: "The Magic Curtain" is from *Passing Through: The Later Poems New and Selected*. Originally in the *New Yorker*. Copyright © 1971 by Stanley Kunitz. Reprinted by permission of W. W. Norton & Company, Inc.

Lehman, David: "Toward a Definition of Love" is from *Valentine Place* (New York: Scribner, 1996). Originally published in *Michigan Quarterly Review*. Copyright © 1996 by David Lehman. Reprinted by permission of the author.

Levertov, Denise: "The Film" is from *Poems 1960–1967*. Copyright © 1966 by Denise Levertov. Reprinted by permission of New Directions Publishing Corporation.

Lindsay, Vachel: "Mae Marsh, Motion Picture Actress" is from *Collected Poems of Vachel Lindsay* (New York: The Macmillan Company, 1925). Reprinted by permission of the Estate of Vachel Lindsey and Simon & Schuster, Inc.

Lowell, Robert: "Harpo Marx" is from *History*. Copyright © 1967, 1968, 1970, 1973 by Robert Lowell. Reprinted by permission of Farrar, Straus & Giroux, Inc.

MacLeish, Archibald: "Cinema of a Man" is from *Collected Poems 1917–1982*. Copyright © 1985 by the Estate of Archibald MacLeish. Reprinted by permission of Houghton Mifflin Company.

Martinez, Dionisio D.: "Reenactments" is from *Bad Alchemy*. Copyright © 1995 by Dionisio D. Martinez. Reprinted by permission of the author and W. W. Norton & Company, Inc.

Matthews, William: "Sympathetic" is from *A Happy Childhood* (Boston: Little, Brown & Company, 1984). Copyright © 1984 by William Matthews. Reprinted by permission of the author.

McClure, Michael: "La Plus Blanche" is from *A New Book/A Book of Torture* (New York: Grove Press, 1961). Copyright © 1961 by Michael McClure. Reprinted by permission of Grove Atlantic, Inc.

McElroy, Colleen J.: "For the Black Rider of the Black Hills and Afternoons of Saturday Matinees at the Antioch Theatre" is from *What Madness Brought Me Here* published by Wesleyan University Press. Copyright © 1990 by Colleen McElroy. Reprinted by permission of the author.

Meltzer, David: "15th Raga/For Bela Lugosi" is from *Ragas* (San Francisco: Discovery Books, 1959). Copyright © 1959 by David Meltzer. Reprinted by permission of the author.

Moss, Howard: "Horror Movie" is from *A Swim off the Rocks* (New York: Atheneum Publishers, 1976). Copyright © 1976 by Howard Moss. Reprinted by permission of the Estate of Howard Moss.

Moss, Stanley: "Prayer for Zero Mostel (1915–1977)" is from *Skull of Adam* (New York: Horizon, 1979). Copyright © 1979 by Stanley Moss. Reprinted by permission of the author.

Moss, Thylias: "Hattie and the Power of Biscuits" is reprinted by permission of the author.

Mura, David: The excerpt from "Pasolini" is from *After We Lost Our Way* (New York: E. P. Dutton, 1989). Copyright © 1989 by David Mura. Reprinted by permission of the author.

Muske, Carol: "Last Take" is from *Red Trousseau*. Copyright © 1973 by Carol Muske. Reprinted by permission of the author and Viking Penguin, a division of Penguin Books USA.

O'Hara, Frank: "Ave Maria" is from *The Collected Poems of Frank O'Hara*. Copyright © 1964 by Maureen Granville-Smith, Administratrix of the Estate of Frank O'Hara. Reprinted by permission of City Lights Books.

Olds, Sharon: "The Death of Marilyn Monroe" is from *The Dead and the Living*. Copyright © 1983 by Sharon Olds. Reprinted by permission of Alfred A. Knopf, Inc.

Oppen, George: "Travelogue" is from *Collected Poems*. Copyright © 1974 by George Oppen. Reprinted by permission of New Directions Publishing Corporation.

Paschen, Elise: "Red Lanterns" (previously unpublished). Copyright © 1995 by Elise Paschen. Used by permission of the author.

Pastan, Linda: "Popcorn" is from *Aspects of Eve*. Originally published in *Mill Mountain Review*. Copyright © 1970, 1971, 1972, 1973, 1974, 1975 by Linda Pastan. Reprinted by permission of Liveright Publishing Corporation.

from *Cavaire at the Funeral.* Copyright © 1980 by Louis Simpson. Reprinted by permission of Franklin Watts, Inc.

Smith, Bruce: "Movies" is used by permission of the author and Sheepmeadow Press.

Smith, Charlie: "Character Part" is from *The Palms.* Copyright © 1993 by Charlie Smith. Reprinted by permission of W. W. Norton & Company.

Smith, Patricia: "Why I Like Movies" is from *Big Towns, Big Talk.* Copyright © 1992 by Patricia Smith. Reprinted by permission of Zoland Books, Cambridge, MA.

Smith, William Jay: "Movies for the Troops" is from *Collected Poems:* 1939–1989. Published in 1990 by Charles Scribner's Sons. Copyright © 1990 by William Jay Smith. Reprinted by permission of the author.

Springsteen, Bruce: "Be True." Copyright by Bruce Springsteen, ASCAP. Reprinted by permission of Jon Landau Management.

Stokes, Terry: "Mentioning James Dean" is from *Crimes of Passion.* Copyright © 1973 by Terry Stokes. Reprinted by permission of the author.

Swenson, May: "The James Bond Movie" is from *Iconographs.* Originally published in the *New Republic.* Copyright © 1969 by May Swenson. Reprinted by permission of the Literary Estate of May Swenson.

Trinidad, David: "Things to Do in *Valley of the Dolls* (The Movie)" is from *Answer Song* (High Risk/Serpent's Tail, 1994). Copyright © 1994 by David Trinidad. Reprinted by permission of the author.

Updike, John: "Movie House" is from *Telephone Poles and Other Poems.* Copyright © 1963 by John Updike. Reprinted by permission of Alfred A. Knopf, Inc.

Villanueva, Tino: "The 8 O'Clock Movie" is from *Scene from the Movie* Giant (Curbstone Press, 1993). Copyright © 1993 by Tino Villanueva. Reprinted by permission of Curbstone Press. Distributed by Consortium.

Voigt, Ellen Bryant: "At the Movie: Virginia, 1956" is from *The Lotus Flowers.* Copyright © 1987 by Ellen Bryant Voigt. Reprinted by permission of W. W. Norton & Company, Inc.

Wakoski, Diane: "Waiting for the New Tom Cruise Movie: Summer '88" is from *Medea the Sorceress.* Copyright © 1991 by Diane Wakoski. Reprinted by permission of Black Sparrow Press.

Walker, Margaret: The excerpt from "On Youth and Age" is from *This Is My Century: New and Collected Poems.* Reprinted by permission of the author and the University of Georgia Press.

Warr, Michael: "Die Again Black Hero: Version II" is from *We Are All the Black Boy* (Chicago: Tia Chucha Press, 1991). Copyright © 1991 by Michael Warr. Reprinted by permission.

Wilbur, Richard: "*The Prisoner of Zenda*" is from *The Mind Reader.* Copyright © 1975 by Richard Wilbur. Reprinted by permission of Harcourt Brace & Company.

Williams, C. K.: "Nostalgia" is from *Poems 1963–1983.* Copyright © 1983, 1988 by C. K. Williams. Reprinted by permission of Farrar, Straus & Giroux, Inc.

Young, Al: "W. H. Auden & Mantan Moreland" is from *The Blues Don't Change: New and Selected Poems.* Copyright © 1974, 1975, 1976, 1977, 1978, 1979, 1980, 1981, 1982 by Al Young. Reprinted by permission of Louisiana State University Press.

Index of Movie Titles and Movie People

Allen, Fred, 87
Alphuville, 61
Arbuckle, Roscoe "Fatty", 87
Arnaz, Desi, 87
Astaire, Fred, 124

Baby Jane, 114
Badlands, 175
Ball, Lucille, 87
Batty, Roy, 104
Bergman, Ingmar, 34, 35
Birth of a Nation, The, 162
Blade Runner, 104
Blow-Up, 171
Bogart, Humphrey, 70, 73
Bond, James, 23
Bow, Clara, 27
Brando, Marlon, 36
Brown, Jim, 67
Bunny, John, 11
Butler, Rhett, 56–57

Cabiria, 11
Casanova, 174
Chan, Charlie, 92
Channing, Margo, 114
Chaplin, Charlie, 7, 11, 87
Cheyenne Autumn, 135–36
Chinatown, 174
Cinderella, 24
Coleman, Ronald, 133
Cooper, Merian C., 46
Cortázar, Julio, 171
Crosby, Bing, 87
Crothers, Benjamin "Scatman", 87
Cruise, Tom, 83

Davis, Bette, 73, 114
Davoli, Ninetto, 152–53
Dean, James, 116, 124, 126
Deer Hunter, The, 175

Dietrich, Marlene, 45, 51
Disney, Walt, 84
Dracula, 39, 86
Dream, Dr., 39

Ekberg, Anita, 55
Enfants du Paradis, Les, 73

Fairbanks, Douglas, 141
Farewell, My Lovely, 174
Fellini, Federico, 55, 174
Fetchit, Stepin, 87
Fields, W. C., 87
Flavia, Princess, 38
Flynn, Errol, 64
Fonda, Jane, 174
Ford, John, 135
Frankenstein, 40

Garbo, Greta, 14
Giant, 125
A Girl of the Paris Streets, 3
Godard, Jean-Luc, 60, 93
Godfather, The, 36
Goldberg, Whoopie, 88
Gone With the Wind, 115, 163
Gorillas in the Mist, 65
Gospel According to St. Matthew, The, 152
Granger, Stewart, 38
Grant, Cary, 87
Greenstreet, Sydney, 78
Griffith, D. W., 11

Hale, Alan, 64
Hardy, Oliver, 87
Harlow, Jean, 71, 90, 171
Hayward, Susan, 156
Helter Skelter, 174
Herman, Pee-Wee, 87
Hope, Bob, 87
How the West Was Won, 151
Hughes, Rupert, 30

Iron Claw, 11

Jezebel, 115

Keaton, Buster, 87
Keaton, Diane, 174
Kerr, Deborah, 38
Keystone Kops, 11
King Kong, 46
King Solomon's Mines, 111
Kinski, Nastassja, 154–55
Kitt, Eartha, 125
Klute, 174
Knife in the Water, 121
Krazy Kat, 36
Kurosawa, Akira, 105

Laurel, Stan, 87
Lipstick, 175
Looking for Mr. Goodbar, 174
Lovely, Louise, 11
Lugosi, Bela, 86

Mabley, Jackie "Moms," 87
Magnani, Anna, 164
Man's Genesis, 3
Man Who Knew Too Much, The, 134
Marsh, Mae, 3
Marx, Harpo, 32, 41
McCarthy, Andrew, 83
McDaniel, Hattie, 163
Mersereau, Violet, 11
Mineo, Sal, 135
Monroe, Marilyn, 27, 107, 157
Moreland, Mantan, 92
Mostel, Zero, 48
Murphy, Eddie, 88

O'Hara, Scarlett, 56–57
Officer and a Gentleman, An, 138
Olive Oyl, 31

Paris, Texas, 154
Pasolini, Pier Paolo, 152
Peck, Gregory, 100–103
Perils of Pauline, The, 10
Poitier, Sidney, 67
Polanski, Roman, 154
Popeye, 31
Power, Tyrone, 133
Pretty, Arline, 11
Prisoner of Zenda, The, 38
Pryor, Richard, 87

Raise the Red Lantern, 176
Rambo, John, 83
Rampling, Charlotte, 174
Rogers, Ginger, 16
Rogers, Will, 87

Saturday Night Fever, 175
Seven Samurai, 105
Seventh Seal, The, 34, 35
Sinatra, Frank, 169
Snow White, 84
Spider Woman, 39
Superman, 79
Sutherland, Donald, 174
Sweet, Blanche, 11

Tarzan, 30, 173
Taylor, Elizabeth, 125
Three Women, 174
Throne of Blood, 109
Trader Horn, 90
Travolta, John, 175
Turner, Ted, 174

Valley of the Dolls, 156

Watermelon Man, 92
Wayne, John, 160
Wharf Rat, The, 3
White, Slappy, 87
Who'll Stop the Rain?, 175
Who's Afraid of Virginia Woolf?, 114
Wild Girl of the Sierra, 3
Williams, Bert, 87
Wizard of Oz, The, 43
Woman Under the Influence, A, 175
Wray, Fay, 46

Z, 150
Zorro, 133

Index of Authors and Poem Titles

"Adonis Theater," 140
"Afterword: A Film," 90
Ai, 124
"American Film, An," 95
Andrews, Tom, 177
Angelou, Maya, 56
Ashbery, John, 54
"At the Movie: Virginia, 1956," 110
"Ave Maria," 49

Baca, Jimmy Santiago, 151
Baraka, Amiri, 67
Bauer, Steven, 134
"Be True," 137
Belitt, Ben, 17
Bell, Marvin, 82
Berrigan, Ted, 72
Berryman, John, 29
"Blond Bombshell," 143
Blossom, Laurel, 113
"Blue Angel, The," 51
Brautigan, Richard, 78
Brock-Broido, Lucie, 169
"Brownsville Girl," 100
Buzbee, Lewis, 173

Carroll, Jim, 147
Carroll, Paul, 55
Castillo, Ana, 154
"Casting Call," 123
"Chaplinesque," 7
"Character Part," 127
"Checkpoint," 113
"Cheyenne," 135
Christopher, Nicholas, 149
"Cinema," 16
"Cinema of a Man," 4
"Cinema Vérité: The River of Barns," 177
Clampitt, Amy, 36
Clark, Tom, 104
Clifton, Lucille, 79
Coleman, Wanda, 123
Coolidge, Clark, 93

Cooper, Jane, 46
Corso, Gregory, 64
Crane, Hart, 7
Creeley, Robert, 53
cummings, e. e., 6

"Dark Palace," 166
"Dear John Wayne," 160
"death is more than," 6
"Death of Marilyn Monroe, The," 107
"Die Again Black Hero: Version II," 162
"Dietrich," 45
Dobyns, Stephen, 98
"Documentary Film of Churchill, A," 19
Doty, Mark, 140
"Double Feature" (Roethke), 13
"Double Feature" (Hayden), 22
Dugan, Alan, 44
Duncan, Robert, 34
Dunn, Stephen, 95
Dylan, Bob, 100

Edson, Russell, 75
"8 O'Clock Movie, The," 158
Emanuel, Lynn, 143
Equi, Elaine, 157
Erdrich, Louise, 160
"Errol Flynn—On His Death," 64

"Farm Film," 54
Fearing, Kenneth, 9
Feldman, Irving, 58
Field, Edward, 45
"15th Raga/For Bela Lugosi," 86
"Film Noir," 149
"Film, A" (Goldbarth), 127
"Film, The" (Levertov), 42
"Final Farewell," 104
"Fission," 146

Fitzgerald, Robert, 16
"For the Black Rider of the Black Hills and Afternoons of Saturday Matinees at the Antioch Theatre," 76
Frost, Robert, 1

Garrigue, Jean, 20
Gerstler, Amy, 172
Ginsberg, Allen, 51
"Godfather Returns to Color TV, The," 36
Goldbarth, Albert, 127
Goldstein, Laurence, 114
Goodman, Paul, 19
Graham, Jorie, 146
Guest, Barbara, 37

Harper, Michael S., 90
"Harpo Marx," 32
Hass, Robert, 105
"Hattie and the Power of Biscuits," 163
Hayden, Robert, 22
"Heroic Simile," 105
Hirsch, Edward, 145
Hollander, John, 63
"Hollywood," 24
"Homage to Film," 29
"Homo Ludens: On an Argument with an Actor," 44
"Horror Movie," 39
Howe, Marie, 144
Hughes, Langston, 8

"Images for Godard," 60
"In a Breath," 2
"Ingmar Bergman's Seventh Seal," 34
"In Person: Bette Davis," 114
"In the Movies," 144

"James Bond Movie, The," 23

"James Dean," 124
Jarrell, Randall, 30
"Jim Brown on the
    Screen," 67
Johnson, Denis, 138

Kees, Weldon, 28
Kerouac, Jack, 41
Kunitz, Stanley, 10

"La Plus Blanche," 71
"Last Take," 119
Lehman, David, 130
Levertov, Denise, 42
"Life Is a Screwball
    Comedy," 87
Lindsey, Vachel, 3
"Living at the Movies,"
    147
"Lost World, The," 30
"Love and Marilyn
    Monroe," 27
Lowell, Robert, 32

MacLeish, Archibald, 4
"Mae Marsh, Motion
    Picture Actress," 3
"Magic Curtain, The," 10
"Main Character," 151
"Making a Movie," 75
"Man Who Knew Too
    Much, The," 134
Martinez, Dionisio D., 171
Matthews, William, 109
McClure, Michael, 71
McElroy, Colleen J., 76
Meltzer, David, 86
"Mentioning James
    Dean," 116
"mesl (male english as a
    second language): in
    defense of
    bilingualism," 133
"Miss Scarlett, Mr. Rhett
    and Other Latter-Day
    Saints," 56

Moss, Howard, 39
Moss, Stanley, 48
Moss, Thylias, 163
"Most Beautiful Blonde in
    the World, The," 157
"Motion Pictures," 37
"Movie" (Rukeyser), 21
"Movie Actors Scribbling
    Letters Very Fast in
    Crucial Scenes," 20
"Movie House," 69
"Movie Run Backward,
    The," 53
"Movie, The"
    (Hollander), 63
"Movie, The"
    (Schulman), 73
"Movie within a Movie,"
    138
"Movies" (Hughes), 8
"Movies" (Ray), 65
"Movies" (Smith), 121
"Movies for the Troops,"
    33
"Mrs. Fanchier at the
    Movies," 9
Mura, David, 152
Muske, Carol, 119

"Necking at the Drive-in
    Movie," 108
"Nostalgia," 81
"note, passed to
    superman," 79

O'Hara, Frank, 49
"Ode to Fellini on
    Interviewing Actors
    for a Forthcoming
    Film," 55
Olds, Sharon, 107
"On Location," 82
"On Youth and Age," 31
Oppen, George, 15
"Or Perhaps It's Really
    Theater," 58

Paschen, Elise, 176
"Pasolini," 152
Pastan, Linda, 70
"Picture," 97
Pinsky, Robert, 97
"Popcorn," 70
"Position without a
    Magnitude," 89
"Prayer for Zero Mostel
    (1915–1977)," 48
"Prisoner of Zenda, The,"
    38
"Provide, Provide," 1

Ray, David, 65
"Red Lanterns," 176
Reed, Ishmael, 87
"Reenactments," 171
"Reunion Banquet, Class
    of '79," 174
Rice, Stan, 108
Rich, Adrienne, 60
Roethke, Theodore, 13
Rudman, Mark, 135
Rukeyser, Muriel, 21

Sadoff, Ira, 118
Sandburg, Carl, 2
Schulman, Grace, 73
Schwartz, Delmore, 27
"Seduced by Natassja
    Kinski," 154
"Seventeen Questions
    about King Kong," 46
Shange, Ntozake, 133
Shapiro, Karl, 24
Shepard, Sam, 100
Shinder, Jason, 166
Shoaf, Diann Blakely,
    74
"Sidney Greenstreet
    Blues, The," 78
Simic, Charles, 89
Simpson, Louis, 43
"Skokie Theatre, The,"
    145

"Slowly I Open My Eyes," 172
Smith, Bruce, 121
Smith, Charlie, 127
Smith, Patricia, 164
Smith, William Jay, 33
"So Long, I've Had You Fame," 169
"Sonnets, The," 72
"Soundstage," 17
Springsteen, Bruce, 137
Stokes, Terry, 116
"Subtitle," 28
"Sunday, Tarzan in His Hammock," 173
Swenson, May, 23
"Sympathetic," 109

"Take One," 118
"Things to Do in *Valley of the Dolls* (The Movie)," 156
"Three Thousand Hours of Cinema by Jean-Luc Godard," 93
"To Harpo Marx," 41
"Toward a Definition of Love," 130
"Travelogue," 15
Trinidad, David, 156

Updike, John, 69

Villanueva, Tino, 158
Voight, Ellen Bryant, 110

"W. H. Auden & Mantan Moreland," 92
"Waiting for the New Tom Cruise Movie: Summer '88," 83
Wakoski, Diane, 83
Walker, Margaret, 31
Warr, Michael, 162
"What You Have Come to Expect," 98
"Why don't you get transferred, Dad?" 43
"Why I Like Movies," 164
Wilbur, Richard, 38
Williams, C. K., 81

Young, Al, 92